Scott's
last expedition

Steve Parker

Published by the Natural History Museum, London

Scott's Last Expedition exhibition is a collaboration between the Natural History Museum in London, Canterbury Museum in Christchurch, New Zealand and Antarctic Heritage Trust New Zealand.

The Natural History Museum and the Antarctic Heritage Trust have been in partnership since October 2005 with the aim raising awareness of historic British Antarctic exploration and the work of the Antarctic Heritage Trust today in conserving the Antarctic historic huts.

The Natural History Museum was instrumental in developing the science strategy for the *Terra Nova* expedition and the vast majority of the specimens collected came to the Museum. Many of the artefacts illustrated in this book are from the Canterbury Museum and the Antarctic Heritage Trust both of which look after artefacts from Antarctic expeditions including the *Terra Nova*, *Discovery* and *Nimrod* expeditions.

For further information see:
www.nzaht.org
www.canterburymuseum.com/
www.nhm.ac.uk/

First published by the Natural History Museum,
Cromwell Road, London SW7 5BD
© Natural History Museum, London, 2011

ISBN 978 0 565 092 870

BASED ON ORIGINAL DESIGN BY David Mackintosh
DESIGNED BY Mercer Design, London
REPRODUCTION BY Saxon Digital Services
PRINTED BY C & C Offset China

FRONT COVER Licensed with permission of the Scott Polar Research
Institute, University of Cambridge

BACK COVER Left: © Herbert G Ponting Canterbury Museum, New Zealand
2009.27.1 (pole), © Canterbury Museum, New Zealand 2009.27.2 (skis).
Right: top © The Wolsey Canterbury Museum, New Zealand 2006.9.1,
middle © Canterbury Museum, New Zealand 2010.10.2, bottom ©
Canterbury Museum, New Zealand 1980.219.1.

CONTENTS

The Expedition

IN THE MIDDLE OF THE NIGHT ON 10 FEBRUARY 1913, the ex-whaling ship *Terra Nova* anchored off the small town of Oamaru, on the southeast coast of New Zealand's South Island. Edward Atkinson, who had been in charge of the Cape Evans base during the last winter, went ashore in a small boat to telegraph breaking news to the world. Its leader Captain Robert Falcon Scott and four colleagues had reached the South Pole just over one year earlier, on 17 January 1912. But they had all perished on the return journey.

So began one of the biggest media events of the twentieth century. One of the greatest tales of heroic adventure from any age was born, with success and achievement overshadowed by failure and tragedy. The British Antarctic Expedition gathered huge amounts of scientific information, from meteorological data, magnetic measurements and glacier observations to large quantities of rocks, fossils and biological specimens. This work added important new knowledge to what was known about Antarctica at the time, and set standards, baselines and benchmarks, some of which are still in regular use today. But the loss of Scott and his Polar Party would dominate public consciousness for months and years to come.

So – who was Scott? Why did he undertake an expedition to the coldest, most remote place on Earth? Were the legends true, and what was the real scientific legacy? Maybe matters could have ended differently.

Robert Falcon Scott
(1868–1912), born in the seafaring centre of Plymouth, England, was a Royal Navy captain and experienced polar explorer. He had already led one venture to Antarctica, the British National Antarctic Expedition of 1901–04.

Before radio and television
broadcasts, the main information carriers were newspapers and illustrated magazines. The Sphere, *in particular, followed the expedition in massive detail with many special supplements.*

THE DISASTER TO THE SCOTT EXPEDITION.

How the Leader and his Four Men Met their Death

"We Bow to the Will of Providence, Determined to do Our Best to the Last."—From the Last Notes of Captain Scott

"Captain Scott and his companions frozen and starved to death"—this was the dreadful fact which gradually formed itself in the minds of the public when the news from the South Pole came through to London and this country. The *Terra Nova*, the expedition's relief ship, returned a full month before her time to New Zealand, but it was not at once learnt at Christchurch that Captain Scott was not on board. Gradually, however, the sinister fact became apparent, and then the news was flashed across the cables in a series of brief messages which were to the following effect :—

"Captain Scott reached the South Pole on January 18 of last year and there found the Norwegian tent and records. On their return [a word here is undecipherable] the southern party perished. Scott, Wilson, and Bowers died from exposure and want during a blizzard about March 29 when eleven miles from 'One Ton' depôt or 155 miles from the base at Cape Evans. Oates died from exposure on March 17. Seaman Edgar Evans died from concussion of the brain on February 17. The health of the remaining members of the expedition is excellent.— E. R. G. EVANS, Commander, R.N."

The news was burst upon London during the afternoon of Monday, February 10, one saffron news bill in particular proclaiming the news with inconsiderate brevity. The news seemed impossible at first to believe, but it came in such a form that doubt could not endure for long. A special meeting of the Royal Geographical Society was at once called, and Parliament and the King immediately took cognisance of this national disaster.

That was the first impression, but soon the feeling gathered force that there was something so bright and shining about the way in which these men met their end—"determined still to do our best to the last"—that in their death they had done a national service which success could scarcely have equalled. The presence of a foreign competitor in the polar quadrant of British endeavour had brought about a curious condition of affairs, intangible and difficult for the general public to follow, but none the less disquieting and unsatisfactory. There was introduced an atmosphere of competition where there should have been none, and where there should have existed an illimitable area of operation there existed a feeling of pressure. The spirit of polar research was in a manner burning dimly. Now with the death of Captain Robert Falcon Scott and his comrades it seems to burn out once again with limpid splendour. High endeavour and fine courtesy again seem possible in the field of polar research.

In this way it seems to us that the little band have again set certain intangible but imperishable things again on their rightful throne. It was a heavy price but it has been paid.

The loss and the price are especially felt by all who knew these polar men at all personally. Captain Scott and his first endeavour in the *Discovery* a dozen years ago had greatly interested this journal. For a long time Britain had taken no part in a field of endeavour in which she had previously been an active participant. Now she was again to enter the field, and the whole expedition was dealt with by this journal in detail from the earliest days when the vessel slipped into the waters of Dundee. The interest of explorers and THE SPHERE gradually became mutual, and the volumes of THE SPHERE which went out to the winter quarters were not unthumbed.

One remembers those departure scenes in London with the vessel warping out on to the heaving bosom of the Thames, and it is with a pang that one realises that the man who led two of these British endeavours now lies buried in an icy tomb far beyond all human habitation. The sun may be shining on it as we write, but soon the snows of winter will be falling again, and who knows when, if ever, the last resting place of Captain Scott will be seen by human eyes ?

North Pole
SIR JOHN FRANKLIN
June 11, 1847

THE TWO WHITE PALLS

Drawn by G. Bron
South Pole
CAPTAIN R. F. SCOTT
March 29, 1912

Mrs. Robert F. Scott with her Son, Peter Scott

Captain Scott married after his return from his first expedition. His wife, who was formerly a Miss Kathleen Bruce, is a clever sculptor and has recently been developing a breeding farm for Siberian dogs

A Nation Mourns

☛ **IT IS DIFFICULT, A CENTURY LATER,** to appreciate the impact of the news that Scott had perished on his return from the South Pole. Norwegian explorer Roald Amundsen and his party had reached this most sought-after goal on 14 December 1911, five weeks before Scott. The Norwegians announced their achievement on returning to Hobart, Australia, on 7 March 1912. So the wider world had been celebrating Amundsen's success for almost one year when news of Scott turned the situation on its head, especially in Britain. There, it dominated the media for weeks and months.

An outpouring of grief accompanied tales of Scott and his group struggling nobly and heroically against the elements, so close to success yet ultimately a fatal failure. The news spread fast throughout the British Empire, whose influence at the time extended to one-quarter of the world's land area and population. British determination had won through and the Empire could be proud of itself. Comparisons with Scott portrayed Amundsen poorly. The Norwegian had enjoyed favourable conditions and had accomplished little in the way of solid science.

The legend grew of 'Scott of the Antarctic', his men not only national heroes but also martyrs to science. But from the 1970s, some began to question events. Were Scott and his comrades really plucky all-British heroes facing insurmountable challenges, especially from the weather? Scott's leadership and judgement, in particular, took a battering. Today, with the centenary of the South Pole conquest, perhaps a more balanced view is emerging.

> '**HAD WE LIVED, I SHOULD HAVE HAD A TALE TO TELL OF THE HARDIHOOD, ENDURANCE, AND COURAGE OF MY COMPANIONS WHICH WOULD HAVE STIRRED THE HEART OF EVERY ENGLISHMAN.**'
>
> **Robert Falcon Scott, March 1912**

News of Scott's death spread *around Britain within hours. A swiftly arranged national memorial service was held in St Paul's Cathedral, London on 14 February 1913, to honour all those who died on the expedition. King George V joined the mourners.*

Antarctica Today

☛ANTARCTICA TODAY IS NOT THE MYSTERIOUS, little-known continent of Scott's day. But it is still the most remote, forbidding place on Earth. Its land area of almost 14 million square kilometres is one and a half times the size of the United States. It has mountains, volcanoes, plateaus and deep canyons. However more than 99% of Antarctica lies hidden under permanent ice and snow, with the ice cap up to almost 4,800 metres thick from the accumulation of hundreds of thousands of years of falling snow. The world's strongest winds and the lowest temperatures are found here. The record is minus 89.2°C in 1983 at Vostok Station, in the centre of the East Antarctic Ice Sheet about 1,300 kilometres from the South Pole. Perhaps surprisingly, Antarctica is also the driest continent. Snowfall is light and the region is regarded as a 'polar desert'. In summer it has round-the-clock daylight; winter varies from twilight to permanent darkness.

On tiny areas of exposed land only limited life-forms are residents. There are various bacteria, cyanobacteria (blue-green algae) and other microbes, and also lichens, some mosses and other simple plants, two flowering plants and over 700 species of algae. Animals range from nematodes and other worms to insects and their relatives, such as midges, lice and springtails.

Visitors to Antarctica include a few seals and birds, especially emperor and Adélie penguins, South Polar skuas, storm petrels and snow petrels. But the Antarctic waters provide a huge resource of food in the summer months. This supports a spectacular variety of wildlife including not only other species of penguins such as chinstrap, macaroni and gentoo, but also blue and killer whales, fur seals, the fabled colossal squid, shrimp-like krill and numerous kinds of fish.

At 3,795 metres, Mount *Erebus is the southernmost active volcano. It is part of Ross Island, off the Antarctic mainland. The base huts of several Antarctic expeditions, including Scott's British Antarctic Expedition, were established on this island.*

Early Expeditions

IN 1773 CAPTAIN JAMES COOK came within 120 kilometres of the Antarctic mainland with the ships *Resolution* and *Adventure*, but sea ice blocked his progress. In 1820 Russian Fabian von Bellingshausen made the first recorded sighting of the continent. The United States Exploring Expedition of 1838–42 named the eastern region Wilkes Land after its commander. British naval officer James Clark Ross headed the British 1839–43 expedition on *Erebus* and *Terror*, naming two volcanoes after his ships and the island was subsequently named after him.

Adrien de Gerlache led the Belgian Antarctic Expedition of 1897–99; his crew included Roald Amundsen. There followed the *Southern Cross* expedition of 1898–1900 under Carsten Borchgrevink, the German South Polar Expedition with German Erich von Drygalski in 1901–03, and Otto Nordenskjöld's 1901–04 Swedish South Polar Expedition. Each added maps, charts and scientific knowledge. Science was important because sponsorship from learned scientific institutions was a significant part of funding.

The British National Antarctic (or *Discovery*) Expedition of 1901–04 was led by Scott himself. Scott, Ernest Shackleton and Edward Wilson marched to within 858 kilometres of the South Pole. Shackleton then headed his own *Nimrod* expedition of 1907–09, and in 1909 came to within 180 kilometres of the Pole.

AGRIOPUS leucopæcilus,
King George's Sound   Sir J. Richardson.

These specimens of a *southern pigfish,* Agriopus *(now* Congiopodus*)* leucopaecilus, *and an emperor penguin,* Aptenodytes forsteri, *were both collected by the Ross expedition of 1839–43.*

James Cook (far left) *narrowly missed Antarctica, then James Clark Ross (left) led a major and successful exploration in 1839–43.*

The Southern Party from *the* Nimrod *expedition of (left to right, below) Frank Wild, Ernest Shackleton, Eric Marshall and Jameson Adams almost attained the Pole itself in 1909.*

Planning

☞ **ROBERT SCOTT HAD NO ANTARCTIC EXPERIENCE** when chosen to lead the 1901–04 *Discovery* expedition. His confidence and naval bearing had impressed Sir Clements Markham, President of Britain's Royal Geographical Society, who recommended Scott for the position. This was the Heroic Age of Polar Exploration. Nations vied to investigate the last great unknown regions on Earth. The Royal Geographical Society was keen to enhance its reputation with major scientific findings doubtless waiting in Antarctica. Plus there was the possible prize of being first to 90°S – the Pole itself. However for the *Discovery* expedition, and for Shackleton's *Nimrod* a few years later, it was not to be.

In 1909, with several Antarctic ventures in the offing, including another by Shackleton, Scott energetically set about raising finance for a new expedition. He wanted a bigger, better return to Antarctica. The estimated cost of £40,000 (about £3.5 million today) was beyond one institution or even the British government. However Chancellor of the Exchequer David Lloyd George agreed that the government would contribute £20,000. The promise of rich scientific rewards attracted the Royal Society, Royal Geographic Society and others, and the services of the British Museum's Natural History department. Supplies and equipment came from sponsors keen to link their names to a South Pole triumph. Scott realized his expedition could appeal to the general public too. He set up all kinds of collections, from gentlemen's clubs to women's institutes and schoolchildren, for the glory of buying a tent, sleeping bag or pony that would ensure a British first to the South Pole.

Cashing in on Antarctica
were hundreds of endorsements, collectables and memorabilia, such as Player's cigarette cards to stick into a commemorative album. This card features a drawing of one of the three ill-fated motor sleds.

More than one hundred
companies and manufacturers donated products and equipment to Scott's Antarctic venture. Of course they ensured their generosity was noted back home. They included Fry's Cocoa and Chocolate, Lyle's Golden Syrup and Tate's sugar – all vital high-energy foodstuffs.

As this carpentry list shows,
all supplies for the expedition were carefully listed and logged with quantities and weights – even down to nails and washers. Leading shipwright on Terra Nova *was Francis Davies of the Royal Navy.*

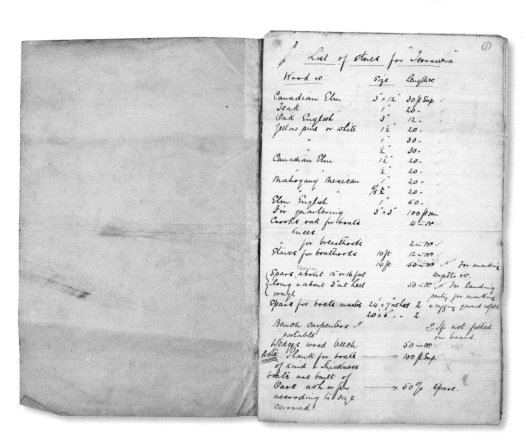

Main Players

☞ **THE BRITISH ANTARCTIC EXPEDITION** is often called the *Terra Nova* after one of its main 'characters'. Built in 1884 *Terra Nova* was a 760-tonne, three-masted, one-steam-engined, ex-whaling and sealing ship. Already a polar veteran, it had helped Scott's *Discovery* vessel get out of the pack ice in 1904. The hull of *Terra Nova* was newly clad with two metres' thickness of oak to protect it against the crushing power of Antarctic ice.

Scott was in many ways the expedition's natural leader. Following the largely successful *Discovery* venture, he was keen to return to Antarctica with the aims of exploring, doing science and reaching the Pole. Previously Scott had risen well enough through the naval ranks. But now in peace time, chances of rapid promotion in the British armed forces were limited. His considerable personal ambition was sharpened by the death of his father, which meant that Scott became sole provider for his mother and two spinster sisters. So he had applied for the *Discovery* expedition and then, with further aspirations for fame and success, planned *Terra Nova*.

More than 60 personnel were selected from some thousands of applicants. Most were naval officers and ratings, including Petty Officer Edgar 'Taff' Evans. From the Royal Indian Marine came Henry 'Birdie' Bowers, and from the army, Captain Lawrence 'Titus' Oates of the 6th Dragoons. There were also non-naval scientific members led by Edward 'Uncle Bill' Wilson, experienced zoologist and illustrator. Both Evans and Wilson had been with Scott on the *Discovery* expedition. These five – Scott, Wilson, Bowers, Oates and Evans – would form the final Polar Party.

'THE MAIN OBJECT OF THIS EXPEDITION IS TO REACH THE SOUTH POLE, AND TO SECURE FOR THE BRITISH EMPIRE THE HONOUR OF THAT ACHIEVEMENT.'

From the Fundraising Leaflet, September 1909

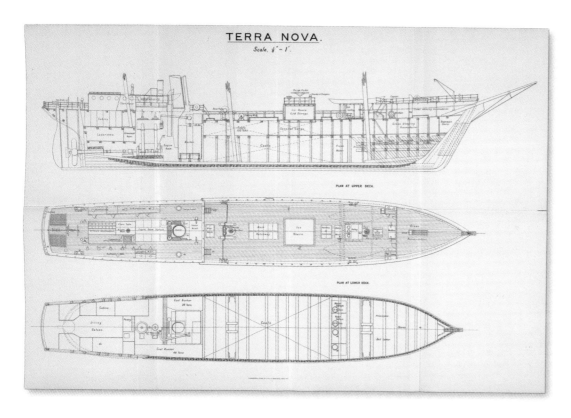

TERRA NOVA.

Scale, ⅜" - 1'.

PLAN AT UPPER DECK.

PLAN AT LOWER DECK.

Terra Nova was 57 metres long and had a 40-horsepower steam engine driving one propeller. At £12,500 it was by far Scott's biggest single purchase for the expedition.

As Terra Nova bid farewell to Australia en route to Antarctica, expedition photographer Herbert Ponting posed the officers, crew and scientific staff on the stern. Scott is front centre, just to the left of the central post.

Setting Sail

(☞) **ON 15 JUNE 1910,** *TERRA NOVA* sailed from Cardiff, Wales to South Africa, then on to Melbourne in Australia, and New Zealand. Scott stayed in Britain to continue fund-raising and organizing, rejoined *Terra Nova* in South Africa, left again in Melbourne and rejoined in New Zealand, always agitating for funds, equipment and publicity.

In Melbourne a telegram arrived that the Norwegian Roald Amundsen and his team, aboard their ship *Fram*, were heading south. *Fram* was supposed to sail to the Arctic, but Amundsen had laid secret plans for Antarctica and the South Pole. Scott understood the implications of this unexpected news but did not alter his plans.

The logistics of preparing for an Antarctic stay of two years or more were huge, even by today's standards. Locally nothing was available except snow, ice, seawater and wildlife such as penguins, seals, seabirds and fish. Everything had to be carried on board, from large prefabricated timber sections and beams for the expedition's base camp hut, to fuel and food, to microscopes and spirit jars for zoological specimens.

Terra Nova left Lyttelton, New Zealand on 26 November, and after picking up Scott and Wilson at Port Chalmers, set sail for Antarctica on 29 November 1910. Throughout the voyage the crew carried out much scientific work. They measured currents and water temperatures at different depths, took seabed soundings and made meteorological and magnetic records. Two days from New Zealand a mighty gale almost sank *Terra Nova*. Ten tonnes of coal, 250 litres of petrol, one of the 33 sled dogs and two of the 19 ponies were lost. Then *Terra Nova* had to fight through heavy ice for three weeks, using another 60 tonnes of coal. It was not all going to be plain sailing.

Specimens were collected *from life* and on paper. *Biologist Dennis Lillie proudly displayed dredged-up large sponges (opposite page), while Edward Wilson treated and prepared the Herald petrel,* Pterodroma arminjoniana, *specimens (above) and made beautifully detailed paintings such as the light-mantled albatross,* Phoebetria palpebrata *(below).*

Arrival

IN LATE DECEMBER 1910, *Terra Nova* finally arrived in the Antarctic. Scott aimed for the shore closest to the South Pole – an ice shelf, now called the Ross Ice Shelf, filling a huge bay with Ross Island at its western end. At the time the ice shelf was known as the Great Ice Barrier. Both the *Discovery* and *Nimrod* expeditions had established huts on Ross Island. Scott decided on a cape 23 kilometres north of his *Discovery* base at Hut Point, and nine kilometres south of the *Nimrod* hut at Cape Royds. He named the new site Cape Evans after his second-in-command.

Unloading began in earnest. Cargo was transported from *Terra Nova* across about two kilometres of sea ice to the base; this took a little over one week. The dogs were overjoyed at their new-found freedom, and the ponies, although terrified at being hoisted off the ship, soon settled in. A third form of transport was three motor sledges, specially developed for the expedition. Two made it ashore safely, but the third broke through a thinning place in the ice and sank.

During the long Antarctic
winter, candles were vital. These Belmont Stearine Candles are actually from the Cape Royds Nimrod hut. Scott's expedition used supplies left there, and used the hut itself as a secondary store for their own items.

Team members man-haul
pony fodder across the sea ice as part of unloading Terra Nova. One of the motor sledges is partly in the picture on the far left.

The Antarctica map shows
the positions of Scott and Amundsen's camps relative to the South Pole, and the places where some of the expeditions from Cape Evans went to.

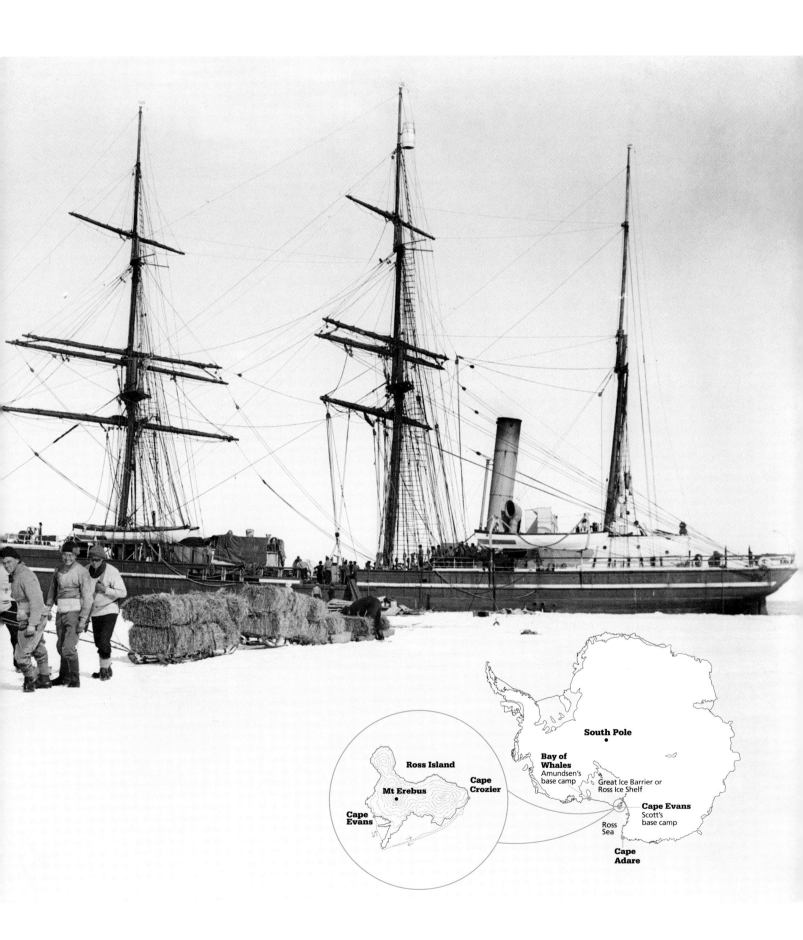

Ross Island

Mt Erebus

Cape Crozier

Cape Evans

South Pole

Bay of Whales
Amundsen's base camp

Great Ice Barrier or
Ross Ice Shelf

Cape Evans
Scott's base camp

Ross Sea

Cape Adare

Setting up Base

WITH THE ANTARCTIC SUMMER FADING, on 17 January 1911 Scott's base hut at Cape Evans was ready for occupation by the expedition's Shore Party of 16 officers and scientists, and nine lower-ranking support members. Scott organized the interior so the upper ranks slept, worked and ate together, while the nine 'men' inhabited the other end. *Terra Nova* soon left, taking its crew and two smaller exploring groups, the Western and Northern Parties, to start their scientific work away from Cape Evans (see pp. 50–55).

The Cape Evans hut, sometimes called Scott's hut or *Terra Nova* hut, was 15 metres long and half as wide. The double-layer planked walls sandwiched a layer of insulating seaweed, while the roof was similar but with three plank layers, and rubber sheets in addition to seaweed. Heating came mainly from the kitchen stove; the main lighting was acetylene gas. Later additions included a utility area 12 metres long, a 3.7-metre-wide porch around one end and pony stabling five metres wide against the long north wall.

The timber hut was not just for sleeping but also for living, cooking, working, relaxing and entertaining. As the Antarctic winter closed in, the dark nights lengthened. June midwinter saw temperatures of below minus 50°C. Going outside was gradually limited to feeding and checking the dogs and ponies, gathering supplies from outbuilding stores, essential scientific work and sporadic exercise.

Inside were beds, bunks and work cubicles. At one end, next to the heating stove, a miniature photographic studio for expedition photographer Herbert Ponting was squeezed between the biology benches of Edward Wilson and his colleagues, and a physics laboratory for Charles Wright and meteorologist George Simpson. At the other end were a galley with kitchen table and shelving for cook Thomas Clissold

'WE HAVE MADE UNTO OURSELVES A TRULY SEDUCTIVE HOME, WITHIN THE WALLS OF WHICH QUIET AND COMFORT REIGN SUPREME.'

Scott's diary, January 1911

The Cape Evans hut plan *shows the science benches and officers' area at one end. The wardroom table dominates the middle, with cooking and accommodation for the 'men' at the other end of the hut.*

On 23 January 1911 team *members were still getting their base in order, as they unpacked, sorted and stored items varying from food cases to sleds and pans.*

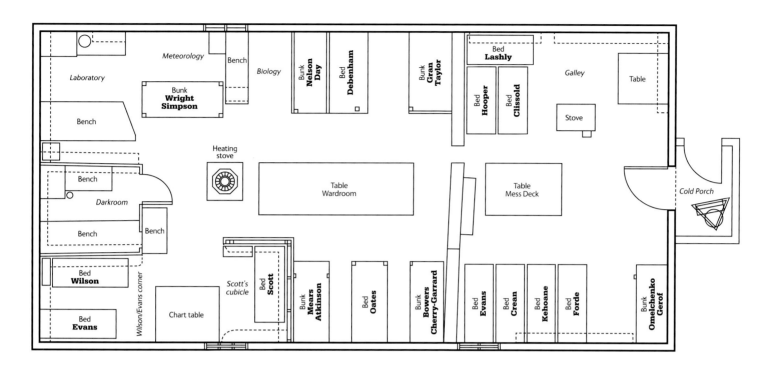

Laboratory	Meteorology		Biology							Bed **Lashly**		Galley	
		Bench		Bunk **Nelson Day**	Bed **Debenham**		Bunk **Gran Taylor**		Bed **Hooper**	Bed **Clissold**		Table
Bench	Bunk **Wright Simpson**											

Heating stove

Table Wardroom

Bench

Darkroom

Bench

Bench

Bed **Wilson**

Bed **Evans**

Wilson/Evans corner

Chart table

Scott's cubicle

Bed **Scott**

Bunk **Mears Atkinson**

Bed **Oates**

Bunk **Bowers Cherry-Garrard**

Table Mess Deck

Stove

Bed **Evans**

Bed **Crean**

Bed **Kehoane**

Bed **Forde**

Bunk **Omelchenko Gerof**

Cold Porch

and a small table for the 'men'. The hut's main focus was the large wardroom table near the middle, next to Scott's 'office'. Here much work, most eating and not a little entertaining took place. Initially the wardroom table was reserved mainly for officers and scientists, while the lower ranks used a smaller table at the other end, opposite the galley. However as time passed and naval protocol gradually relaxed, especially when Scott was away, all the men mucked in and ate or worked where they could.

Setting up his base was one of Scott's most satisfying events during the whole expedition. He wrote: 'We have made unto ourselves a truly seductive home, within the walls of which quiet and comfort reign supreme.'

In their row of bunk beds, *nicknamed 'The Tenements', Oates (upper left) chats with Cecil Meares while Atkinson takes a break below.*

Clissold's cramped galley *area was packed high with provisions, but cooking went on daily regardless – here rolling dough for pies.*

Provisions

☛ **APART FROM MEAT AND OIL HARVESTED FROM SEALS**, penguins and fish, and seabird eggs, everything edible for the whole expedition was brought on board *Terra Nova*. Scott and his colleagues spent months meticulously planning which provisions to take, using the experiences of previous expeditions. Among their supplies were large quantities of high-energy foods in concentrated or dried forms, stored in tins with lift-off lids or sealed-lid cans.

The planning for food and provisions was not just for meals in the hut. There were frequent minor expeditions lasting a few days, where 'sledging rations' applied. Longer treks, including the Northern and Cape Crozier Parties (see pp. 52 and 57), also needed provisioning. And of course there were food and supply depots to be laid for the southwards journey to the Pole itself. Each of these ventures had specific lists of foodstuffs, built around the most up-to-date nutritional advice on ingredients, nutrients and calories.

As well as staples and the occasional departure from daily fare, there were some luxury items to lift the spirits on important dates. These included the significant Antarctic midwinter solstice on 21 June to mark the longest night, which was also celebrated as Christmas. There were also birthdays and personal anniversaries. At these times wines, spirits with soda mixers, champagne, Christmas pudding, asparagus, plum pudding and other treats were comforting reminders of life continuing in the wider world.

Scott's notes recall that hot *cocoa was one of the most anticipated drinks. He had visited the factory of a cocoa producer back in Britain to thank the staff personally for their donations of money and supplies.*

Malt drinks were an *important part of the evening routine. Tinned malt kept its flavour and energy content well. It could also be added to other foods and drinks to enhance the taste.*

Occasional 'treat' foods *included tinned fish such as salmon steaks and several kinds of cheeses, often imported. Flavourings such as salt were also available, as well as a variety of spices and sauces.*

Catering

☛ **MEALTIMES WERE CENTRAL EVENTS** in the Cape Evans hut routine. The men discussed ongoing plans for their diets, energy requirements in calories, and what was and was not known about the dreaded effects of scurvy. Its actual cause, lack of vitamin C, was not clear at this time – 'tainted meat' was one suspect. But prevention of scurvy by fresh fruits and vegetables was recognized – although these were not an option for two years in Antarctica.

Expedition cook Thomas Clissold and his rota of assistants were charged with using every scrap of food. This was rationed and the amounts used at every meal were carefully measured to avoid items running out. One of the chief chores was baking fresh bread almost daily for all 25 men. To let himself know when the dough had risen, so that he never overcooked and wasted food, Clissold rigged up a contraption whereby the rising dough tripped a mechanism that made a bell ring and a lamp glow. It was just one example of the endless ways in which Scott's team members tinkered, modified and adapted what they had for what they wanted. In fact this work was Clissold's original trade. He was a skilled mechanic and tradesperson or artificer in the Royal Navy, and had learned to cook as a second career in order to be selected for the expedition. Later he gave valuable assistance in using the motor sleds during their short life.

While the 'men' had plain *cutlery, enamel mugs and jugs, the officers and scientists enjoyed finer dining. There were also higher-class items such as soup tureens and cruet sets, decorated with the expedition emblem.*

Scott heads the table for *his 43rd birthday on 6 June 1911. It was very close to midwinter, so spirits were raised by an excellent meal, plenty to drink, and pennants decorating the hut.*

Daily Routine

☞ **TO AVOID BEING FROZEN IN FOR THE WINTER** *Terra Nova* had left Cape Evans and Antarctica by early February 1911. The ship headed back to New Zealand, loaded with its first batch of reports, specimens and letters for home, and those onboard continued their scientific work on the way. The Shore Party settled in for their first Antarctic winter.

Scott kept a watchful eye on his men as he supervised affairs in and around the Cape Evans hut. For example, he was keen that everyone should have some fresh air and outdoor exercise even in the depths of winter. So despite the bone-chilling temperatures, he encouraged after-lunch outdoor groups to carry out routine jobs or simply stretch their legs and arms. Ponting the photographer was especially reluctant to go outdoors and Scott remarked that he 'liked the fire better'. Occasionally it was necessary physically to drag him from the hut to enjoy the benefits of fresh air and exercise.

Apart from routine catering, tending to the ponies and dogs, and preparing for the next summer with its trek to the Pole, the greatest calling during the long months of darkness was science. Specimens of rocks and fossils were examined and catalogued. Conditions were recorded several times daily at weather stations set up by the team, including air and ice temperature, atmospheric pressure, wind speed and snowfall. Scott appreciated the value of this scientific work to the overall success of the expedition. He often asked questions of the scientists, and sometimes puzzled at the immensely detailed notes and records, but he rarely interfered.

A battery-powered telephone *system and aluminium wires linked Cape Evans to Hut Point more than 20 kilometres to the south. The first calls between the two were made on 6 October 1911.*

Sewing was part of regular *servicing and maintenance, especially for tents, sleeping bags and clothing, on which lives depended. Everyone was responsible for his own kit. Here Edgar Evans machines new seams onto a tent.*

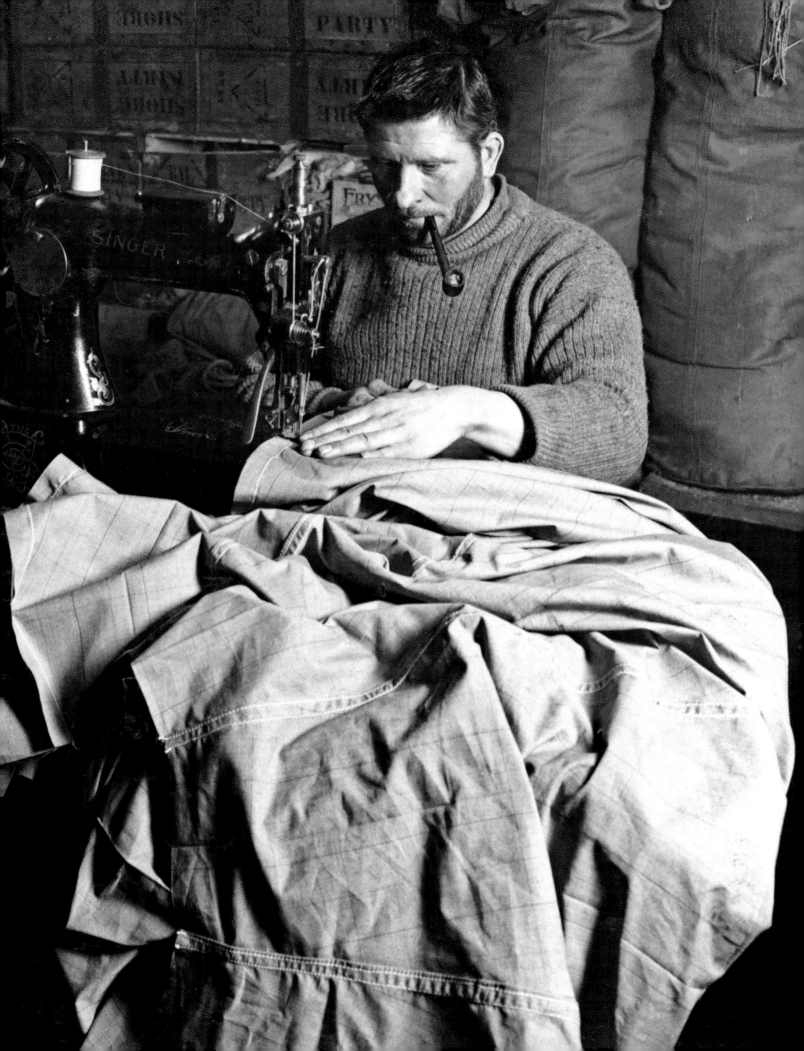

Clothing

LONG BEFORE THE DEVELOPMENT of the breathable, high-tech fabrics used for today's cold-weather clothing, Scott and his men had their own versions. Before the expedition, Scott had organized tests on canvas, wool, various leathers and other materials, treating them with different oils and potions to see if these improved insulation, waterproofing and durability. But there was still a reliance on natural materials such as hides and furs from reindeers and seals for use as gloves and some footwear.

For the most part, expedition members kept warm and moved around easily. Each man worked out his own preferences and adapted his clothes to suit. The main problem was not keeping out the cold and wet, but rather the sweat caused by exertion, especially when man-hauling sledges. Sweat soaked from the inside outwards and compromised insulation. Removing layers to dry near a fire was one answer. This system worked well in the Cape Evans hut but was less successful on expeditions for fieldwork, sledging by day and in tents by night. Then the wearer had to work quickly after removing gloves and mittens. If the fingers became damaged, adjusting clothes was then virtually impossible.

Some observers criticized Scott's use of woollen garments below the outer layer, saying that natural furs would have been better suited to avoid the effect of excess perspiration, especially when man-hauling.

Ski-type boots, worn for *sledging and general outdoor work, received lavish and detailed care. This pair possibly belonged to, or were worn by, Scott himself.*

Outer garments included *the hooded, windproof jacket, worn over several upper-body layers, and thin oilskin over-trousers covering ordinary trousers and longjohns. This jacket (far left) was worn by Scott's second-in-command Edward Evans, member of the final support party to turn back, who almost died on return to Cape Evans.*

Among the undergarments *were the important long johns with their convenient front flap, and thick cotton shirts (left). This shirt belonged to physicist Charles Wright, who did much outdoor prospecting and surveying.*

Healthy Living

☛ **THE *TERRA NOVA* MEMBERS WOULD BE OUT OF** touch with civilization, including doctors and hospitals, for months at least, and probably years. They were selected for the expedition with their basic fitness and health in mind, and also for their ability to look after themselves. A tiny cut might become infected, or a slight injury out on the ice could endanger survival. Hence the need for serious attention to personal care, health and hygiene at all times.

The expedition's chief medic was Edward Atkinson. He trained at St Thomas' Hospital, London, and joined the Royal Navy in 1908. His main interests were research orientated, especially parasitology. Part of his brief was to examine all team members regularly and dispense drugs as necessary from the relatively sophisticated (for the time) medical kits at the Cape Evans hut, and to supply the mini-kits carried on sledging trips. Among the medications one might raise eyebrows at today – opium tablets. They were to be used as painkillers and were carried on some sledge outings, including the final Polar Party's march, and were also for use 'in the event that conditions become intolerable'.

Each man was responsible for personal requirements such as a toothbrush, hair brush and shaving equipment. Washing of men and their clothes usually took place near the main stove in the hut. Clothes were dried on a clothes' horse in front of this with rotas preventing a log-jam of laundry.

Edward Atkinson, here at *his biology bench in the hut, spent much time looking for parasites – not so much among the men, but inside fish, penguins, seals and other animals that had been collected and dissected.*

This hand mirror was *beautifully framed in sealskin by dog-driver Demetri Gerof.*

Soaps and detergents were *used both for washing and as a wax-like lubricant for outdoor mechanisms such as machinery and sled runners. This particular bar is from the Nimrod hut at Cape Royds.*

Toothbrushes, in an age *before plastics, generally had bone handles. This example was left behind in the Cape Evans hut, then reused by Dick Richards during Shackleton's Imperial Trans-Antarctic Expedition of 1914–17.*

Shave or not? The Royal *Navy allowed either a full beard or a cleanly shaved face. Scott took his personal shaving brush and remained clean shaven.*

Leisure Time

☞ **ALTHOUGH CRITICISMS HAVE BEEN LEVELLED AT SCOTT** over his failings during his push for the Pole, no-one can fault his awareness of the need for leisure time and activities to divert attention from daily routines, hardships and deprivations. During the long winter months in the hut, most evenings were enlivened by some kind of arranged event, from music recitals to lectures, mini-theatre plays, photographic viewings and games. Expedition photographer Herbert Ponting showed lantern slides and also played the banjo and sang, to a mixed reception. The scientists would speak about their current work and findings, and advise the others to look out for certain kinds of rocks, clouds or ice formations. Several of the men's diaries mention that the expedition's gramophone gave many hours of pleasure and entertainment – not just the recorded music discs it played, but also the construction and quality of the machine itself, and how it worked. Obtaining sounds from a wavy groove in a flat disc was state-of-the art audio technology.

When the weather was reasonable, Scott organized outdoor activities such as football matches. There was also the inevitable rough-and-tumble, and occasional practical jokes such as hiding a shaving brush or wrapping a 'surprise' in a shirt – like a dead fish. Each man took his selection of favourite books and these were lent around, becoming more dog-eared as winter progressed. There was much informal chat about scientific and support work, and plans for the coming summer's trip to the South Pole.

Scott's gramophone was *a Monarch Senior model, introduced in 1905. It had an oak case and brass-barrelled, triple-spring clockwork motor. Its makers, The Gramophone Company, lent the device to Scott and later welcomed it back – still in working order.*

Books such as Steele Rudd's For Life *were eagerly shared among team members, who would offer their own critiques and compare notes after reading.*

Letter-writing was an *important and rewarding pastime. This message from Able Seaman James Paton, member of the ship's party, is on emblem-headed notepaper.*

This pack of advert-carrying *playing cards sits in a case signed by Petty Officer Edgar Evans, who accompanied Scott to the South Pole. Several new card games were invented during the long winter days and nights.*

Herbert Ponting's projected *slides were of his travels, a reminder of the world outside, sometimes reassuring but occasionally upsetting the men with thoughts of home.*

A Long Winter

☞ **DURING THE LONG ANTARCTIC WINTER OF 1911**, the men gradually got to know each other's personalities, likes, dislikes, strengths and weaknesses. They were mostly confined to the hut, where conditions were crowded with limited personal space. Some close friendships were forged, and occasional tensions surfaced. Chief scientist Edward Wilson's calm, considered manner earned him the nickname 'Uncle Bill' and he became a confidant of several of the men, including Scott. In fact Wilson was probably the only true confidant for Scott, who tended to value his privacy and remain aloof.

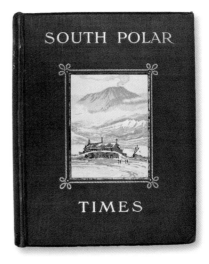

A Cape Evans publication called the *South Polar Times*, edited by Apsley Cherry-Garrard, kept the mood light. It carried amusing articles, scientific pieces, general interest, not a few jokes, and illustrations showing varied levels of skill. The *South Polar Times* was started by Scott himself in 1902 on his *Discovery* expedition, with Ernest Shackleton as editor. Shackleton went one step further by producing a full book on his *Nimrod* expedition.

Also during the 1911 winter, any excuse was taken to stage some kind of event or distraction. Midwinter in June 1911 was enlivened by 'Christmas' presents and toys including cigars, and a popgun for Lawrence Oates who declared: 'If you want to please me very much, you will fall down when I shoot you.'

Cherry-Garrard's office *experience came into its own with the writing and editing of reports and production of the in-house publication.*

The *South Polar Times* was *a periodical first produced during Scott's earlier Discovery expedition. It was revived for Terra Nova and served to occupy wandering minds and hands.*

This menu in the shape *of an emperor penguin was handmade by biologist Edward Nelson, for the second Midwinter's Day dinner held at Cape Evans on 22 June 1912. Decorations included an improvised Christmas tree from bamboo in a pot of gravel.*

Much importance was *placed on food for special events. Supplies included 450-gram (one-pound) tins of asparagus – no less than 400 of them, some specially imported into Britain from the Netherlands.*

As a warming flavour, *ginger was loved by some and loathed by others. Requests for individually tailored meals, unless for medical reasons, usually received short shrift.*

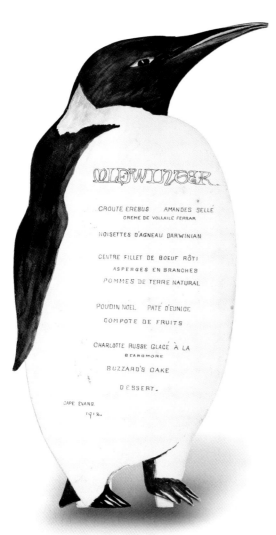

On the shifting pack ice,
*Harry Pennell sights formations
and takes a compass bearing,
to measure the ice drift and
its deformation. As captain on
Terra Nova,* Pennell was well
suited to magnetism studies.

Science Outside

👉 **DESPITE THE MAIN AMBITION TO REACH THE POLE,** key aims of the *Terra Nova* expedition were its scientific and exploration programmes. These were built on the experience and knowledge of previous expeditions such as *Discovery* and *Nimrod*, but with a leap in scope and quantity, and the expedition greatly furthered scientific knowledge about Antarctica.

When planning the expedition, with advice from backers and learned institutions, Scott had appointed his *Discovery* comrade Edward Wilson as chief scientist. The two then selected members for the science party according to the different skills they possessed. Some were recruited because they were recommended by eminent scientists of the time. Others wanted desperately to go and had applied themselves. Canadian-born Charles Wright walked from Cambridge to London to demonstrate his enthusiasm and offer his services in person to Scott. He was taken on as physicist.

The variety and breadth of the scientific programme were astonishing. Work was conducted in geology, glaciology (a branch of science that was in its infancy), magnetism, chemistry and physics studies, meteorology, and many aspects of biology. One relentless set of recordings was the weather. Several types of thermometers were used for the temperature of the air, ice and rocks, and the water at different depths. Wright spent many hours sketching and recording ice and iceberg formations and also studying heat and radiation from rocks.

Antarcticoxylon (Rhexoxylon) priestleyi, *named after expedition geologist Raymond Priestley, shows life once thrived on Antarctica. The thermometer was taken to Antarctica by the* Nimrod *expedition, then reused by Charles Wright.*

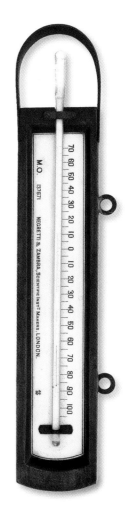

Science Inside

☛ **THE SCIENCE AREAS OF THE CAPE EVANS HUT** were usually a hive of activity. Specimens were brought back, studied, described, catalogued, treated, preserved and stored, ready to be sent back on *Terra Nova*. Everyday activities involved dissecting animals such as fish, seals, seabirds and penguins, preparing specimens such as feathers, fur, skins and bones, selecting the best geology specimens, sketching and photography. Microscope work included studying minerals and crystals in rock formations, examining samples of seawater and melted ice for microbial life, and looking at tiny parasites in larger animals. Some microscopes were taken outside the hut to look at snow and ice in minute detail, and on treks. Record books gradually filled up with notes that would become the basis of the expedition's formal scientific reports. All this was done in cramped conditions near one end of the hut.

The team was a mixture of highly qualified scientists, such as the geologists T. Griffith Taylor, Frank Debenham and Raymond Priestley, and men with little to no scientific experience. Cherry-Garrard, a graduate in Classics and Modern History from Oxford who was seriously short-sighted, twice offered his services, the second time with a donation of £1,000; he was twice rejected. When he handed over the money in any case Scott and Wilson were so impressed that they took him on as assistant biologist – despite no polar experience and little scientific knowledge. However Cherry-Garrard's enthusiasm and skills with writing and secretarial work made him an invaluable team member.

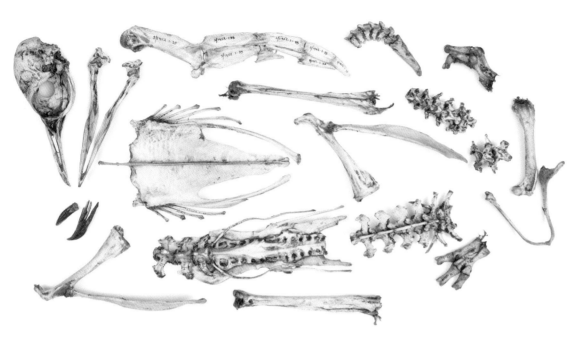

Edward Wilson's microscope, *used mainly in the hut, was one of several types on the expedition. Atkinson used his to study parasites found in fish and penguins. Small portable microscopes were also taken on treks away from the hut.*

These bones represent the *skeleton of an Adélie penguin, probably the most common penguin species along Antarctic shores. Methods of removing, cleaning and preserving animal bones were well developed.*

Biologist Dennis Lillie's notes *record which specimens were packed where; Antarctica's Lillie Glacier is named after him.*

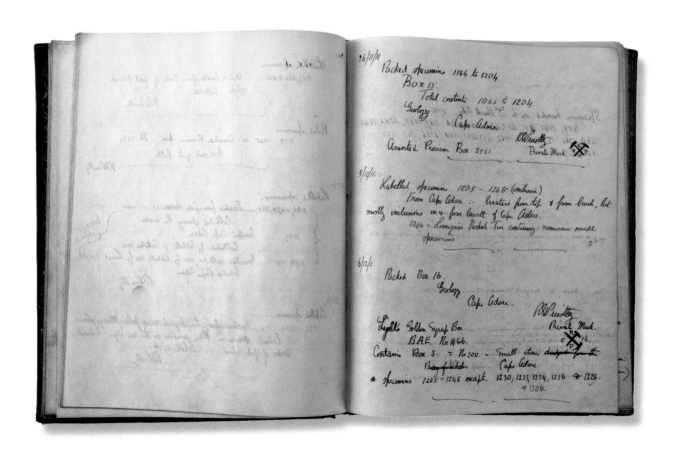

Specimens Galore

☛ **SOME OF THE MATERIALS AND SPECIMENS** collected on the *Terra Nova* expedition involved great personal hardship – none more so than on the Cape Crozier venture (see p. 57). Also it took time and experience to choose the best items for packing and returning to Britain. Often, finding a new specimen in excellent condition and much more representative of its kind, meant rummaging through packing crates and storage boxes so that it could replace an earlier version. Many species were completely new to science and took years to classify and name back in Britain.

The brittle- or basket-star, Astrotoma agassizii, *is an ophiuroid, a cousin of starfish within the echinoderm group. This one was collected at McMurdo Sound off Ross Island. The species is now known to be common around Antarctica and nearby islands.*

Lichens such as *Buellia* frigida *are among the commonest organisms on the cold, bare rocks of Antarctica. They are combinations or partnerships of fungi with either algae (simple plants) or microbes called cyanobacteria (blue-green algae).*

Isopods are types of *crustaceans, along with krill, prawns and crabs. Familiar small isopods on land are woodlice and pillbugs. Much bigger marine types include* Glyptonotus antarcticus. *This specimen, collected from North Bay, Cape Evans, is in a jar 15 centimetres high.*

This 26-centimetre-long *skull of a Weddell seal,* Leptonychotes weddellii, *shows its fearsome, dog-like teeth. A sizeable seal, three metres long and weighing perhaps half a tonne, it is one of the most southerly ranging of all mammals.*

Ponting's array of cameras *included this Prestwich cinematographic camera – what we would now call a movie or video camera. With this type of equipment he captured sequences of daily life, landscapes, seascapes, and also animals and their behaviour for scientific records.*

Photography

☞ **OFFICIAL PHOTOGRAPHER HERBERT PONTING** was one of the oldest members of the *Terra Nova* expedition. Talented and experienced, he had worked as a miner and fruit-grower in the United States' 'Wild West' before turning to photography, and covering wars and other assignments across Asia. As well as still photographs, Ponting was also a cinematographer and was one of the first to use a portable movie camera in Antarctica.

Ponting regarded himself as a 'camera artist'. He documented most aspects of expedition life, from the initial *Terra Nova* voyage until he left on board the same ship some 14 months later, in March 1912 (as Scott's party were returning from the South Pole). His thoughtful composition and careful framing for the camera often involved his subjects posing for minute after minute. This caused much under-the-breath muttering and team members invented their own verb, 'to pont', referring to keeping still for long periods.

Photographic film was available but Ponting preferred to use the old-fashioned glass plates. In the hut he worked with the temperamental magnesium-based 'flash candles' of the day. He also took some autochrome plates – an early type of colour system that yielded the first colour photographs of the 'white continent'. He returned with a total of 1,700 photographic plates that form an incredible record of work and life onboard *Terra Nova* and at Cape Evans.

Ponting's work contributed greatly to the expedition's scientific achievements and its iconic status today. He also trained several others in photography especially Australian geologist Frank Debenham, and before his departure passed on some of his cameras.

Ponting's skis were among *the least used. He was somewhat infamous for avoiding strenuous outdoor travel.*

Illustrations

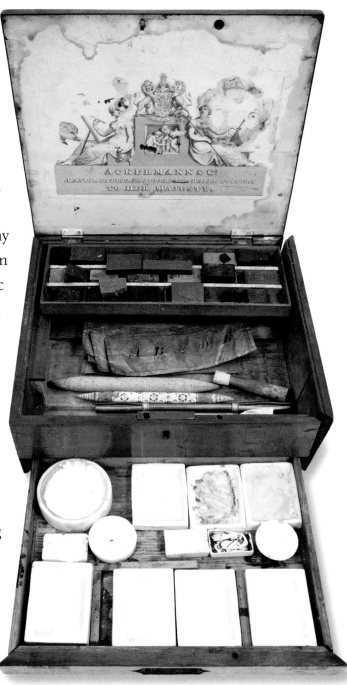

☞ **EDWARD WILSON** was a veteran of Scott's *Discovery* expedition and, with Shackleton, its attempt on the South Pole in 1902–03. Chief scientist and artist on *Terra Nova*, he had developed his childhood interest in nature and drawing into a First Class degree in Natural Sciences from Cambridge, and a distinguished career as a naturalist and illustrator. Then he attended St George's Hospital Medical School, London, and qualified as a physician.

Terra Nova was the first Antarctic foray where photography featured so prominently. Previously the emphasis had been on artists creating the visual records. Even so, the scientific illustrations of Wilson and others were, with the photographs, an integral part of record-keeping and were included in the huge volume of reports. Wilson's watercolours captured perfectly the desolate, brooding grandeur of Antarctica's land- and seascapes. Many of his sketches and watercolours were heavily scientific, working with the collected specimens to portray the animals and their behaviour when alive. Often he made sketches outside, with a written record of colours, then worked on the painted details back in the Cape Evans hut.

Wilson encouraged others in the group, including invertebrate zoologist Edward Nelson, to develop their illustration skills. Deeply religious and thoughtful, Wilson was a close friend to many team members and probably the nearest thing to a soulmate for Scott, who wrote: 'Words must always fail me when I talk of Bill Wilson. I believe he really is the finest character I ever met.'

Oct. 18. 1910.

Oct. 18. 1910.
Sept. 3. 1910.

Oct. 20. 1910.

*Cf. Lillie "Terra Nova" Rep.ᵗ, p.122, Pl. viii, fig.ˢ 2–4
(Lagenorhynchus obscurus, Gray)*

This paint box was returned *to Wilson's sister Ida in Britain and contains paints from the original set as well as additions made by Wilson himself. The mixing trays show the remains left behind from making up colours. He mainly painted indoors but on the occasions when he did this outdoors, Wilson used a thermos of warm water to prevent his brushes from freezing.*

Wilson's artistic output *was enormous, and he varied his illustration media and detail according to the task in hand. The dusky dolphins,* Lagenorhynchus obscurus, *are formal identification-type colour portraits. The sketchbook page shows crabeater seal,* Lobodon carcinophaga, *behaviour demonstrating postures and movements.*

Communications

THE *TERRA NOVA* EXPEDITION PRODUCED huge amounts of written and pictorial records – far greater than any Antarctic venture before it. These varied from personal jottings, diaries and letters home to casual notes about the Cape Evans hut, journals from the sledging treks, scientific notes and sketches. There were also official catalogues, forms and records to fill in, especially for the scientists and those responsible for keeping track of stores and equipment. The coming and going of *Terra Nova* meant that, in effect, there was just one annual post back home.

The scientific material, both reports and actual specimens, eventually returned to Britain, to institutions such as the Department of Natural History of the British Museum and the Royal Geographical Society, and various university research departments. Here it was pored over and written up into about 80 official reports.

Scott, keen on gadgets and cutting-edge technology, had explored taking radio equipment to Antarctica. Amundsen worried about this, reasoning that even if Scott reached the Pole second, but then radioed the news, he would grab the headlines first. However early radio equipment was vastly cumbersome and unreliable, and Scott dropped the idea. Instead, the expedition made do with a Royal Mail postal service. This had perhaps the most infrequent collection of any British 'Post Office', since winter ice meant that *Terra Nova* visited only in the summer to resupply the Shore Party and take away specimens, reports and letters.

will be the final, but I should not be surprised to stay here 2 years we shall for certain if we are not successful this year, and possibly if we are please remember me to the wife & daughter and excuse this scribble we hardly have a moment to ourselves we are all the old boys wish to be remembered to you with best wishes I conclude Sincerely Yours Taff

Cape Evans
Ross Island
Antarctic
23-1-11

Dear Charlie

a few lines to let you know that I am in the best of health and hope this will find you the same we have settled here at last quite close to our old quarters, only 8 miles away, so the surroundings are quite familiar to us all we tried to land at

The Cape Evans 'Post Office' *stamp bore the legend BRIT. ANT. EXP. (British Antarctic Expedition). The type set in the box lent an official feel to the mail, even though it was collected so infrequently, and letters (left) were headed with the expedition emblem.*

Scott is photographed *writing his journal, in October 1911. To his right on the wall are pictures of his wife Kathleen and son Peter.*

Heading West

☛ **THE *TERRA NOVA* EXPEDITION** included several expeditions. The longest and most famous was the trek to reach the South Pole itself. Other secondary expeditions varied from a few days to many months, and most had exploration, science and surveying as their main tasks. As with the main polar march, some were full of astonishing drama, immense difficulty and dreadful deprivation. They are amazing adventure stories in themselves – all in the name of science. Unlike the South Pole trek, however, none of them involved loss of life.

Two such expeditions were the Western Geological Parties. The first commenced soon after the Shore Party had settled into Cape Evans and lasted from 27 January to 14 March 1911. T. Griffith Taylor and Frank Debenham, both Australian geologists, Charles Wright and Petty Officer Edgar Evans made up the party. *Terra Nova* crossed McMurdo Sound, the large bay west of Cape Evans and Ross Island, and left them at Butter Point where they surveyed and collected specimens along the Ferrar Glacier, Dry Valley, Taylor Glacier and Koettlitz Glacier. Their march back went smoothly to Hut Point but then was delayed by shifting sea ice and it was another month before they reached Cape Evans. Like several of the sub-expeditions, they carried some specimens back but left the bulk to be collected by *Terra Nova* at the end of the whole Antarctic stay.

The second Western Geological Party set out the next summer, in mid-November 1911, to explore farther north. Taylor, Debenham, Norwegian ski expert Tryggve Gran and Robert Forde travelled across sea ice to Granite Harbour, north of Butter Point, and continued exploring, surveying and gathering specimens along the Mackay Glacier. Ice prevented *Terra Nova* from picking them up on 15 January, so on 5 February the men began a desperate march back. Luckily *Terra Nova* picked them up two weeks later, still over 200 kilometres from Cape Evans.

Known as Beacon sandstone
(opposite top), this specimen is from Granite Harbour, one of the Western Geological Party sites. Once sea bed, it contains fossils of warm-water creatures from 250–400 million years ago. This showed that Antarctica had drifted from higher latitudes.

Studying crystals in
specimens such as this hornblende–biotite granite, from the Flatiron Headland near Granite Harbour, McMurdo Sound, allows geologists to estimate how and when the rocks of Antarctica formed.

Dark-coloured kenyte lava
is found in only two places: around Mount Erebus in Antarctica, and around Mount Kenya in Africa.

The second Western
Party arrived back at Cape Evans dishevelled and weatherbeaten: (from left) Forde, Debenham, Taylor and Gran. Their home for almost two months was Stone Hut at Geology Point.

East Then North

☛ **SOON AFTER THE CAPE EVANS BASE WAS ESTABLISHED,** and after dropping off the first Western Geological Party, *Terra Nova* then turned around and headed in the opposite direction with the Eastern Party, led by keen skier and Royal Naval Lieutenant Victor Campbell. They sailed along the edge of the Ross Ice Shelf or Great Ice Barrier, hoping to explore Edward VII Land at its eastern end. (This region was named in 1902 by Scott's *Discovery* expedition.) But Campbell found the ice too dangerous to land and they turned around to sail west, back along the shelf edge. Their alternative was to travel past Ross Island to explore the region at the other end of the Ross Ice Shelf, Victoria Land. However not far along, in a curved inlet in the shelf called the Bay of Whales, they met Roald Amundsen.

Amundsen and his team had arrived there on *Fram* about one week after *Terra Nova* reached Cape Evans. They set up their base Framheim ('Fram Home') on the ice shelf some four kilometres from its sea edge and began preparations, like Scott, for a Pole trek late in the year. Equally surprised, the British and Norwegians exchanged pleasantries and visited each other. Campbell soon reasoned that *Terra Nova* should return swiftly to Cape Evans with the important news. This they did, but Scott himself was away laying depots for the Pole trip, so Campbell left messages. Then on 9 February 1911 the Eastern Party became the Northern Party and set off on its second option to Cape Adare at the tip of Victoria Land.

On 20 February 1911 *Terra Nova* deposited the Northern Party of Campbell, Harry Dickason, Raymond Priestley, G. Murray Levick, Frank Browning and George Abbott near Cape Adare, more than 700 kilometres from Cape Evans. They built a hut and endured the 1911 Antarctic winter and next brief summer, carrying out surveys and gathering specimens. But their work was limited by unfavourable ice and no route inland.

This extraordinary meeting of Fram *(in the foreground) and* Terra Nova, *in an otherwise vast and empty ocean, occurred on 3 February 1911 in the Bay of Whales. Each crew was courteous, offering tours of their ship and meals. But underlying tensions showed they all had the same goal.*

Almost a year later in early January 1912, *Terra Nova* brought fresh supplies and took them south to Evans Coves, 320 kilometres from Cape Evans. The planned pick-up was six weeks later but *Terra Nova* could not penetrate the severe sea ice. In mid April, Atkinson led a party from Cape Evans, where it was now assumed that Scott's Polar Party had perished, to try and reach the Northern Party, but the weather was too severe. Campbell and his five comrades realized they were stranded, facing a second Antarctic winter with just four weeks' food. They dug a snow cave on Inexpressible Island and planned their survival. They spun out their slim rations with fish, penguins and seals, burned seal and penguin blubber in an adapted stove, and treasured their single set of clothing. It is difficult to imagine such desperate conditions, yet they made it. On the 7 November 1912, they arrived back at Cape Evans after a trek of six weeks in a severely weakened state and began their recovery.

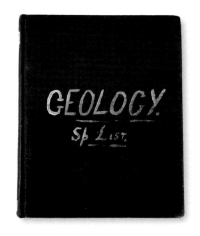

Australian geologist
Raymond Priestley's notebook lists hundreds of specimens collected by the Northern Party.

This anemometer (wind *speed indicator) was used by the Northern Party at Cape Adare. In one blizzard the anemometer registered 135 km/h, then broke.*

Just arrived back at base, *exhaustion and deprivation are etched into every aspect of the Northern Party: Dickason, Campbell, Abbott, Priestley, Levick and Browning.*

The Worst Journey

☞ **SURVIVING AN ANTARCTIC MIDWINTER** is difficult enough in a purpose-built hut. No wonder that some *Terra Nova* personnel regarded the Cape Crozier scientific outing as madness. The Cape had been named in 1841 by Ross's expedition on *Erebus* and *Terror*, after Captain Francis Crozier of *Terror*. Cape Crozier was at the eastern end of Ross Island, the other end to Cape Evans. Chief scientist Edward Wilson planned a 'Winter Journey' trek there – almost 100 kilometres through the darkness and plummeting temperatures – to collect birds' eggs!

But not just any birds' eggs. They were from emperor penguins, *Aptenodytes forsteri*, the largest of the penguin species, 120 centimetres tall and weighing more than 40 kilograms. Wilson had seen their

This view of Cape Crozier, *with its forbidding cliffs, was taken from* Terra Nova *during the warmer months of 1911. In midwinter the entire scene was icebound and of course dark.*

Wilson, Bowers and *Cherry-Garrard tuck into a well-earned meal back at Cape Evans, having endured some of the worst conditions on Earth in the name of science.*

breeding colony at Cape Crozier on the *Discovery* expedition and his aim was to collect eggs at different stages of development and examine the embryos inside. This was connected with a theory at the time that penguins, and emperor penguins in particular, were the most primitive or ancestral of all birds. Following Darwin's evolutionary theory, penguins might have evolved from reptile ancestors millions of years ago – perhaps even dinosaurs. So early embryos of penguins might pass through a reptile-like stage in their development, as a recapitulation of their distant evolution.

Emperor penguins breed in the depths of winter, hence Wilson's 'Winter Journey'. He and Scott added another aim to the trek – to test sledges, clothing, food rations and other aspects of polar travel in the very worst conditions. Bowers and Cherry-Garrard agreed to accompany Wilson and on 27 June 1911, a few days after midwinter's day, they set off.

For 19 days in darkness, with temperatures at times below minus 60°C, Wilson and his two colleagues struggled to Cape Crozier. They encountered deep snowdrifts, jagged ice blocks, crack-like crevasses, howling gales and blizzards. On some days they covered barely two kilometres and they had only a tent for shelter and everything was iced through. Yet they were able to reach a site near the colony and build an igloo-like shelter from stones. Reaching the actual colony, only just more than six kilometres away, was still terribly difficult but eventually the trio collected five emperor penguin eggs. On the return to the shelter two of these broke. The embryos of the remaining three were removed from the shells and put into alcohol when they got back to Cape Evans.

If conditions were not already awful enough, a blizzard raged from 22 July ripping the roof off their shelter. It also blew away their tent, which was being used for storage, but was vital for the return journey. Wilson, Bowers and Cherry-Garrard huddled in their sleeping bags, singing and telling jokes as the snow whipped around. At last a lull allowed them to find their tent, lodged in rocks about 800 metres away, and they rapidly prepared to trek back. On 1 August, almost five weeks after leaving, they walked back into Cape Evans.

55 Series
Emperor Penguin

74. Series
Emperor Penguin

64. Series
Emperor Penguin

A Kodak film canister was *re-used to hold pebbles taken from the stomach of an emperor penguin, possibly swallowed to adjust the bird's ballast in the water.*

The paraffin (kerosene) *hurricane lamp provided vital light on the Cape Crozier trip, which was endured in almost total darkness.*

The three emperor penguin *eggs collected by Wilson and his colleagues on 20 July 1911 are still in the collections of the Natural History Museum in London. They were presented to the Museum in 1913 by Cherry-Garrard.*

The 'Winter Journey' *emperor penguin embryos were cut into about 800 thin slices, stained, and put onto glass slides for microscope study. Their official scientific report did not appear until 1934, by which time ideas about bird evolution had changed.*

The backpack carried *specimen bottles and emergency supplies during shorter excursions.*

Push for the Pole

☛ **IN 1911 THE HEROIC AGE OF ANTARCTIC EXPLORATION** was reaching its climax. The South Pole was the greatest quest of the age. Both Scott's *Terra Nova* and Amundsen's *Fram* teams had arrived in early 1911, with similar plans to attain this goal. First, use the end of the summer, January and February, for depot-laying. This involved setting up depots – stores, camps or caches – of supplies such as food, fuel and equipment, at sites on the way to the Pole, as far as conditions would allow. Next, sit tight through the winter, preparing equipment and perfecting plans. Finally, attempt the main polar trek as soon as possible when the next summer began, late in 1911. Scott's base at Cape Evans was about 1,450 kilometres from the South Pole. Along the edge of the Ross Ice Shelf, in the Bay of Whales, Amundsen's base Framheim was in straight-line terms some 110 kilometres closer.

There were differences in the approaches of the two expeditions. Members of the *Terra Nova* expedition carried out huge amounts of scientific work including environmental recording, surveying and collecting. Amundsen and his men did little apart from what was needed to navigate and survive on their 'dash to the Pole'. From both his own *Discovery* and Shackleton's *Nimrod* expeditions, which were also based on Ross Island, Scott had considerable information about the obstacles in his way. Amundsen had much less knowledge about his route, but the Norwegian's team was more streamlined, relying on sledges pulled by dogs. Scott was juggling with four modes of transport to haul his sledges – petrol engines, ponies, dogs and men.

Scott kept this photograph *of his wife Kathleen in his cubicle at the Cape Evans hut. The couple had married in 1908 and had a baby son, Peter. Kathleen travelled as far as New Zealand to wave her husband goodbye as* Terra Nova *set off for Antarctica.*

Wright (foreground) and *Bowers carefully test-pack sleds in preparation for the South Pole journey.*

With Mount Erebus in the *background, Scott (slightly forward, left of centre) and the members of the Polar Party and support parties are ready to depart for 90°S.*

Ready To Go

☞ **SOON AFTER THE ARRIVAL OF *TERRA NOVA*** in January 1911, depot-laying began. The general plan was to send out sledges loaded with supplies and deposit these at suitable intervals southwards. It was hurried work since in just a few weeks the all-too-short Antarctic summer would fade as the cold and darkness closed in.

Before today's GPS system, navigation was based on latitude and longitude. Latitudes are imaginary west–east circles around the Earth, from the equator at 0° to the North Pole at 90°N, and the South Pole at 90°S. They, and corresponding north–south lines or longitudes, were obtained by reading times, directions and angles between the sun, other heavenly objects such as the moon and prominent stars, and the horizon, using scientific instruments such as the chronometer and sextant. Each one degree of latitude represents a distance of 111 kilometres on the ground. Both Scott and Amundsen used these

readings not just for navigation but also for depot-laying. Amundsen planned ten depots, first at each degree from 80° to 85°S, then less frequently. Scott aimed for 12 depots, with 'Last Depot' to be set at 89°S during the final push to the Pole.

From Cape Evans, Scott established early depots at what he regarded as suitable intervals, using his own *Discovery* experience and what he had read of Shackleton's plans. He incorporated landform features and established Safety Camp and Corner Camp, and Bluff Depot at 79°S. Then, running out of time and with the ponies in a dreadful state, at almost 79.5°S – nearly half a degree, or 48 kilometres, short of the intended 80°S – he ordered all remaining supplies to be left as One Ton Depot. Named because of their weight, the depot was just over 260 kilometres from Cape Evans. Of the eight ponies involved in depot laying, only two survived. Falling short of 80°S would have major consequences for Scott's return journey from the Pole.

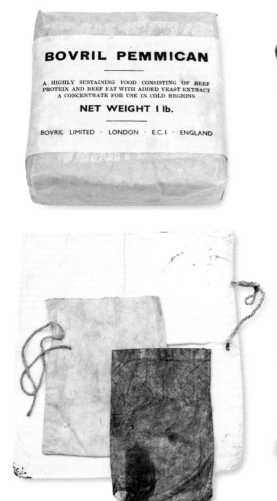

Bowers, Atkinson and *Cherry-Garrard cut and weigh pemmican, from cans on the table, to make up individual sledging rations.*

This map of the route to *the South Pole was featured in Cherry-Garrard's* The Worst Journey in the World, *1922. About half the trek was across the 'Barrier', now known as the Ross Ice Shelf.*

There were various recipes *for pemmican, a concentrated mixture of dried meat and fat or lard. Sometimes it also contained cranberries providing vitamin C, but the brands used on the expedition did not. On the South Pole trek the rations per man per day included 340 grams of pemmican, 450 of biscuits, 57 of butter, 85 of sugar, 16 of cocoa and 24 of tea.*

Hundreds of ration bags, of *several sizes and designs, were used to carry food on sleds. Rations for one day for one man or dog were pre-sorted and put into bags for the trip. Empty bags were used for innumerable purposes, such as holding scientific and geological samples.*

Amundsen

☛ **ROALD AMUNDSEN ORIGINALLY HOPED TO BE FIRST** at the North Pole. Then in April 1909 he heard that, allegedly, it had been achieved by American Robert Peary – a claim still hotly disputed today. Having planned a big expedition, Amundsen decided to switch Poles. His ship *Fram*, meaning 'forward', left Norway in August 1910. It was supposed to head south through the Atlantic Ocean, around South America's Cape Horn, then north to the Pacific Arctic. But on a mid Atlantic stopover in Madeira on 9 September, Amundsen and his senior officers informed the men of their changed plans. They would keep going south to the Antarctic and the South Pole.

The *Fram* expedition's camp Framheim was in the Bay of Whales, on the Ross Ice Shelf, far from Scott's base. Amundsen's previously planned venture to the North Pole was supposed to be very scientific and the ship carried equipment for observation, recording and collecting. But when he decided to head south, Amundsen reduced these scientific aspects of the expedition. Some of the science equipment was not loaded at all, and much of the rest was not even unloaded at the Bay of Whales. It stayed aboard *Fram* as the ship left before the Antarctic winter for an arranged oceanographic survey voyage.

Reaching the South Pole became Amundsen's sole aim. Like Scott, the Norwegians laid depots as far south as possible before the winter of 1911, reaching 82°S. During the darkness they worked on their equipment, replanned their strategy and route in increasing detail, and practised loading and unloading the sleds so they could set up camp with speed and ease.

'**VICTORY AWAITS HIM WHO HAS EVERYTHING IN ORDER – LUCK, PEOPLE CALL IT. DEFEAT IS CERTAIN FOR HIM WHO HAS NEGLECTED TO TAKE THE NECESSARY PRECAUTIONS IN TIME. THIS IS CALLED BAD LUCK.**'

Roald Amundsen

Amundsen's originally
'over-engineered' sledges were modified during the winter at Framheim. The team shaved away unnecessary wood to make them less than two-thirds the weight but with virtually no loss of strength.

Amundsen shows off his
cold-weather clothing, based on natural furs, and his tailor-made skis, in this photograph from 1912.

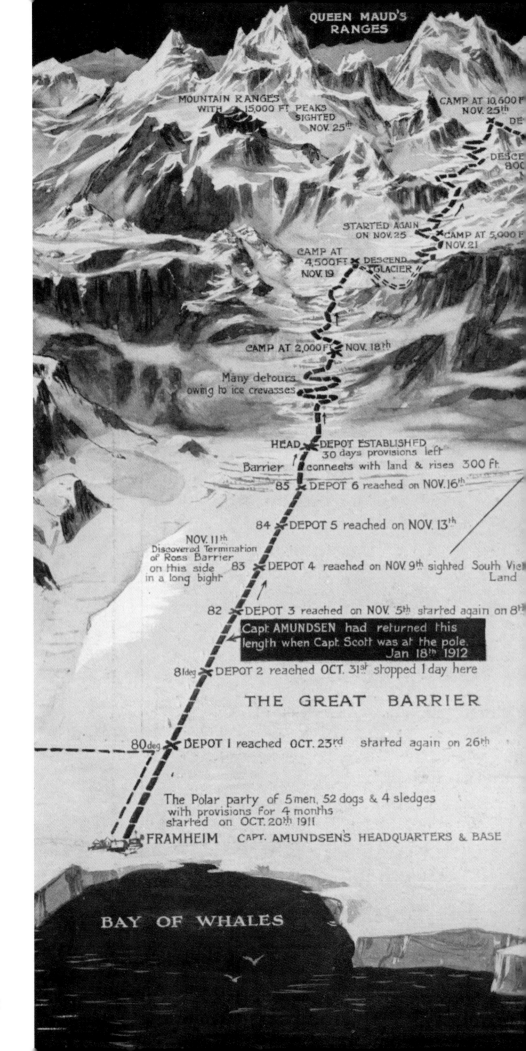

QUEEN MAUD'S RANGES

CAMP AT 10,600 ft NOV. 25th

DE

DESCE 800

MOUNTAIN RANGES WITH 15,000 FT PEAKS SIGHTED NOV. 25th

STARTED AGAIN ON NOV. 25

CAMP AT 5,000 F NOV. 21

CAMP AT 4,500 FT NOV. 19 DESCEND GLACIER

CAMP AT 2,000 FT NOV. 18th

Many detours owing to ice crevasses

HEAD DEPOT ESTABLISHED 30 days provisions left

Barrier connects with land & rises 300 ft.

85 DEPOT 6 reached on NOV. 16th

84 DEPOT 5 reached on NOV. 13th

NOV. 11th Discovered Termination of Ross Barrier on this side in a long bight

83 DEPOT 4 reached on NOV. 9th sighted South Vie Land

82 DEPOT 3 reached on NOV. 5th started again on 8th

Capt. AMUNDSEN had returned this length when Capt. Scott was at the pole. Jan 18th 1912

81deg DEPOT 2 reached OCT. 31st stopped 1 day here

THE GREAT BARRIER

80deg DEPOT 1 reached OCT. 23rd started again on 26th

The Polar party of 5 men, 52 dogs & 4 sledges with provisions for 4 months started on OCT. 20th 1911

FRAMHEIM CAPT. AMUNDSEN'S HEADQUARTERS & BASE

BAY OF WHALES

Both Scott and Amundsen
had similar overall routes to the South Pole, although the Norwegians' Framheim base at the Bay of Whales was just over 100 kilometres closer than Cape Evans. 'The Great Barrier' was the name at the time for the Ross Ice Shelf or Great Ice Barrier.

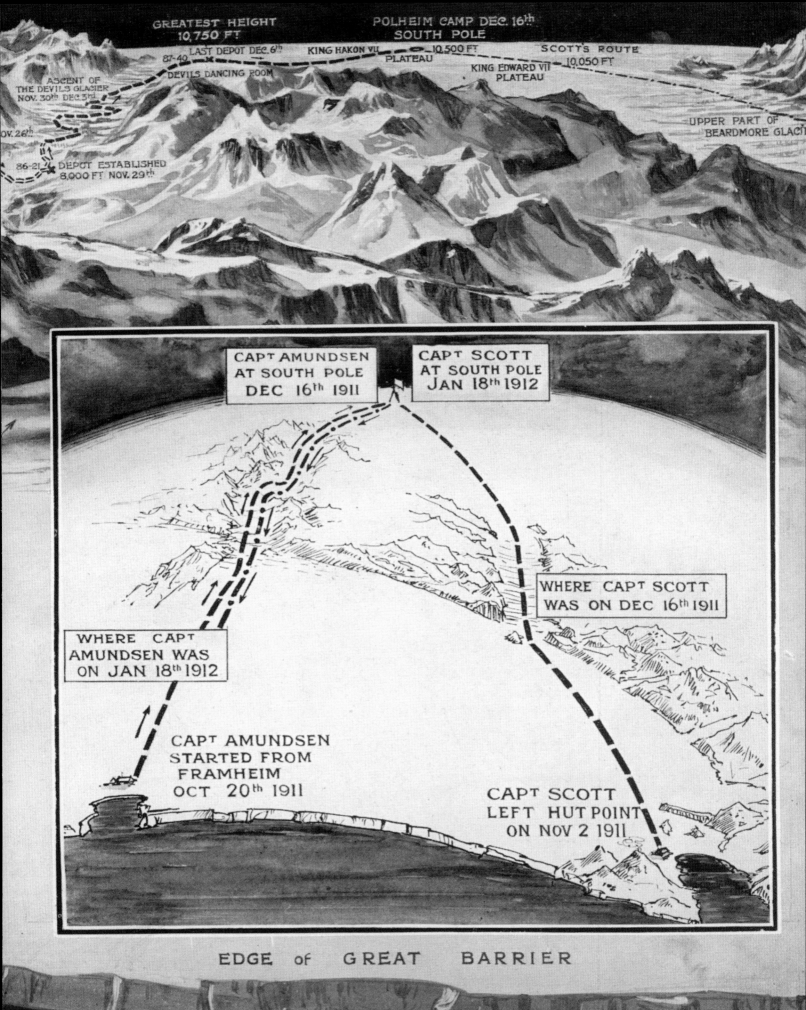

GREATEST HEIGHT
10,750 FT

POLHEIM CAMP DEC. 16th
SOUTH POLE

LAST DEPOT DEC. 6th   KING HAKON VII   10,500 FT   SCOTT'S ROUTE
87-40   PLATEAU
DEVILS DANCING ROOM   KING EDWARD VII   10,050 FT
PLATEAU

ASCENT OF
THE DEVILS GLACIER
NOV. 30th DEC. 3rd

UPPER PART OF
BEARDMORE GLACI...

NOV. 26th

86-21   DEPOT ESTABLISHED
8,000 FT NOV. 29th

CAPT AMUNDSEN
AT SOUTH POLE
DEC 16th 1911

CAPT SCOTT
AT SOUTH POLE
JAN 18th 1912

WHERE CAPT SCOTT
WAS ON DEC 16th 1911

WHERE CAPT
AMUNDSEN WAS
ON JAN 18th 1912

CAPT AMUNDSEN
STARTED FROM
FRAMHEIM
OCT 20th 1911

CAPT SCOTT
LEFT HUT POINT
ON NOV 2 1911

EDGE of GREAT BARRIER

Equipment

THE EXPERIENCES OF DEPOT LAYING, the 'Winter Journey' to Cape Crozier and other outings around Cape Evans all furnished Scott with further information for the great South Pole trek. He planned food rations, and practised skiing and sledge pulling by the technique called man-hauling. Each member of the journey was responsible for care and repair of his clothes and other individual equipment, and could modify these to his personal preferences.

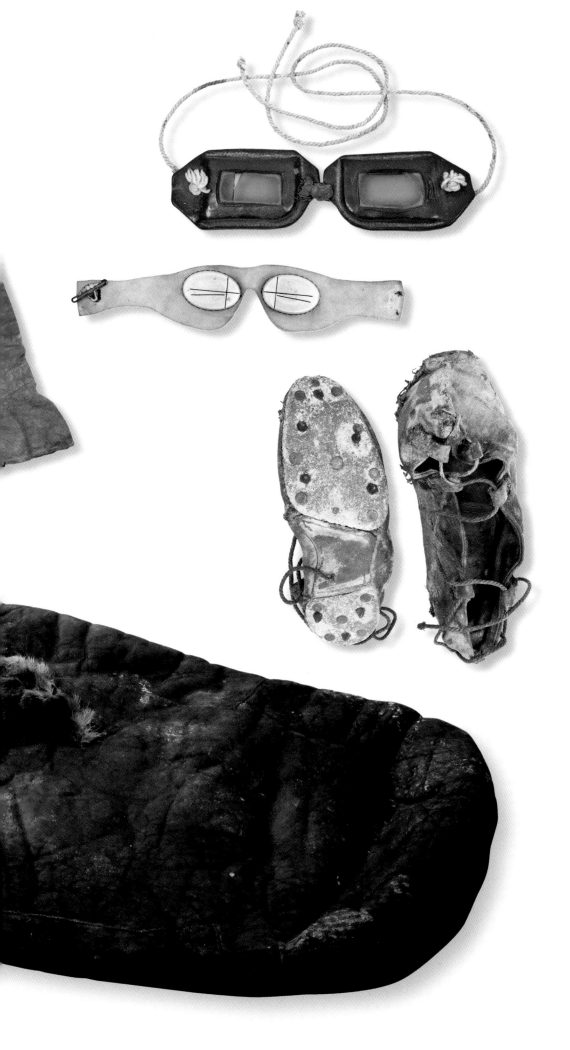

This is Cherry-Garrard's *sledging balaclava for the Cape Crozier expedition. Like many items of clothing it was adapted by the wearer with a fur-lined windproofed piece across the nose that gave, according to Cherry-Garrard, 'the greatest comfort'.*

Reindeer fur, which has *hollow hairs, was favoured for sleeping bags. Smooth fur from the animal's flanks lined the inside, while the two outside flaps were of softer, woollier belly fur. Warm and comfortable when dry, the bags could be four times heavier when iced up from condensation in tents.*

Standard-issue leather-and- *glass goggles, here as used by Lashly, protected against snow, its blindness causing glare and the intense cold. Some men took other goggle designs, such as the aluminium slit-eyepiece type.*

This crampon style was *the most successful in the expedition. The lower sole has two aluminium alloy plates studded with four-pointed nails to grip the ice, fixed to a thick leather sole with canvas sides. Cords threaded through side eyes fitted the crampon under the boot.*

Pony Power

☞ *TERRA NOVA'S* **SIBERIAN PONIES** were bought by chief dog-handler Cecil Meares for the sum of £5 each in Manchuria, now northeast China. Meares' original mission was to buy dogs; when asked by Scott to purchase ponies, he admitted he knew little of them. When Oates, a cavalry officer, saw them he knew at once they were in poor condition but Scott overruled Oates' concerns. As pony feed was loaded on the ship, a worried Oates bought an extra two tonnes of hay himself.

The ponies were relatively successful in helping to unload *Terra Nova*. But as soon as depot laying began, their limitations were severely exposed. They sank deeply in snow, struggled in the wind and slipped on ice. Depot laying was beset by blizzards, falls into crevasses, and terrified ponies belly-deep in slush and ice, kicking and struggling in vain, or even being

threatened by the hungry dogs. Matters worsened for them when the main Polar Party set off in November 1911. The surviving ponies' fates were sealed as meat for men and dogs.

The motor sledges fared even worse. One of the £1,000 machines, made specially by Birmingham's Wolseley Tool and Motor-Car Company, sank while being unloaded from the *Terra Nova*. The others needed constant coaxing and adjustment. As the main Polar Party got under way a second machine, driven by Bernard Day, broke down with a cracked cylinder not far from Cape Evans. The third, with driver William Lashly, made it to Safety Camp, 80 kilometres from Cape Evans, and then died. Scott maintained he had never depended greatly on the motor sledges – their job was partly done, as high-tech publicity for the expedition's fundraising.

Dogged Work

FOR *TERRA NOVA*, 33 SLEDGE-PULLING DOGS were bought for the sum of £1/10 shillings each under the supervision of chief dog handler Cecil Meares. Charged by Scott to procure them, Meares travelled to Nikolayevsk in Siberian Russia for the task. While there he fell in with expert dog driver Demetri Gerof, who was also recruited for the expedition. Along with the ponies, which he bought on the same trip, Meares supervised the transfer of the animals to Japan and then New Zealand and *Terra Nova*.

Meares and Gerof took care of the dogs and helped Oates with the ponies. They were all used during depot laying in early 1911 and then at the start of the main South Pole trek from Cape Evans in November. The dogs could be unruly, barking and running to and fro so that their

pulling lines or traces became hopelessly tangled. They also chased penguins and other birds and had fights among themselves – they were in effect several wolf-like packs with submissive members challenging to lead a group or split one into two. Once a group of dogs even attacked one of the ponies when it collapsed from exhaustion.

Scott was not an expert in dog driving, but he had experience of their capabilities and planned to use them where possible. However he did not feel that he could rely on them alone, hence the ponies and motor sledges; harsh experience soon showed him that the dogs were far better suited to hauling sledges and provisions. On the main trek to the South Pole the dogs were used effectively until man-hauling became the only mode of transport.

Osman, the expedition's *lead dog, had been financed by Richmond School, Yorkshire. He was washed overboard during the* Terra Nova's *gale encounter, then miraculously swept back onboard.*

This dog bootie was perhaps *an experiment to protect ice-cut paws as they healed. Dogs, like ponies and men, suffered greatly from frostbite, snow blindness, harness chafing and stomach complaints.*

Cecil Meares prepares a *loaded sled for dog-hauling. Meares oversaw the care and welfare of the dogs with Gerof.*

Man-Hauling

AS WINTER FADED IN MID-SEPTEMBER, Scott announced his plans for the South Pole. He discussed very little with the others, even Wilson, tending to come to decisions by himself. He proposed tackling the first stage of the journey, crossing the Ross Ice Shelf, with 16 men plus all transports. On reaching the Beardmore Glacier, one party with dogs would turn back. The ponies would be shot and their meat used as food on the return. Then, man-hauling all the way, three groups of four would continue. Man-hauling meant pulling laden sleds by means of a harness around the shoulders and abdomen. Scott regarded this as a tried and tested method when compared with using animals or motorized contraptions, and relished the physical challenge. As the groups progressed from the Beardmore Glacier, one and then a second would return to base, leaving a final foursome for Pole.

The man-haul harness, made *from webbing, fitted around the front of the body with straps over the shoulders. It was attached to a manilla rope passed through an eye on the sled's front, secured by a wooden toggle.*

For sledging journeys, *Wilson designed a medical case for a unit of four men. It weighed 1.8 kilograms and contained drugs and medical supplies for most ailments the men might encounter. This example was carried by the search party that found the bodies of Scott and his companions.*

Starting the sledge to gain *momentum was the most difficult phase of man-hauling. It often needed helpers to overcome the stuck sledge.*

Heading South

☛ **THE POLAR PARTY AND SUPPORT GROUPS** left Cape Evans from late October, with the last group leaving at the start of November 1911. This was later than they had expected as they had to wait for suitable conditions for the ponies. With motor sledges, dogs, ponies and man-haul teams proceeding at different speeds, progress was a logistical nightmare complicated by blocks of ice, soft snow, howling winds and unseen crevasses. After the Ross Ice Shelf came the steep Beardmore Glacier, one of the world's largest at more than 160 kilometres long. Discovered by Shackleton's *Nimrod* expedition, it was named in honour of Sir William Beardmore, Scottish industrialist and expedition sponsor.

By 9 December the last five ponies had been shot and their meat cached, then the dogs returned. It was now men only. On 21 December Scott selected another support party to return – Cherry-Garrard, Atkinson, Wright and Patrick Keohane. On 4 January 1912 the final support party did the same, but three men returned rather than four – Edward Evans, Thomas Crean and William Lashly. For some reason Scott wanted five for the final 240 kilometres to the Pole. On 9 January he remarked that passing Shackleton's 'Furthest South' was one of the most uplifting events.

Evans, Crean and Lashly faced their worst calamity on their 1,200-kilometre trek back to Cape Evans. Evans fell ill and collapsed. Lashly stayed with him while, on 18–19 February, Crean walked 56 kilometres non-stop in 18 hours on a few biscuits and chocolate, from Corner Camp to Hut Point for help. Atkinson and Gerof were there, provisioning and waiting for return groups. Evans was saved, although he had to leave on the next *Terra Nova* departure for proper medical care.

The aluminium Nansen cooker had an outer and inner pot on a circular tray, above a paraffin-fuelled primus with an aluminium windshield. The whole apparatus packed into itself to save space. A properly set-up Nansen cooked a meal for four in around 40 minutes.

Cigarettes and pipes were a common way of relaxing, as well as getting stimulation from the nicotine. (This was 40 years before the full harm of smoking was revealed.)

Sledging biscuits were packed into sealed tins to make them watertight, suitable for depots and easy to pack. Scott recorded that fewer biscuits were taken on the South Pole trip than he intended, reducing daily rations still further.

The long ice pick was made of polished wood and metal, and the sledge of wood, leather and rope. Sledges had minimal structure to save weight, and axes were used for specimen-collecting as well as travel.

Bitter Success

☛ **ON 16 JANUARY 1912, SCOTT AND HIS FOUR COLLEAGUES** spied a black marker flag against the relentless white. Their hearts sank. It was one of many flags set out in various directions by Amundsen's party. Amundsen had made dozens of sightings with sextants and other equipment, and sent men up to 20 kilometres in several directions, to leave flags and make sure at least one of them was at the true Pole.

Next day, 17 January 1912, the British found Amundsen's tent Polheim, or 'pole home', near what they estimated to be the South Pole. Inside were letters to the King of Norway and other items. The Norwegians had arrived 34 days before, on 14 December 1911, and stayed for three days. (Amundsen's recorded arrival was 15 December but he had not accounted for crossing the International Date Line.) When Scott's party arrived, the Norwegians were well on their way back. Travelling at up to 50 kilometres per day – two or three times Scott's average speed – they arrived back on 26 January 1912. Their whole South Pole trek took 99 days. With little equipment and few scientific specimens to load on the ship, by 30 January *Fram* had left Antarctica for Tasmania.

'DEAR CAPTAIN SCOTT – AS YOU PROBABLY ARE THE FIRST TO REACH THIS AREA AFTER US, I WILL ASK YOU KINDLY TO FORWARD THIS LETTER TO KING HAAKON VII. IF YOU CAN USE ANY OF THE ARTICLES LEFT IN THE TENT PLEASE DO NOT HESITATE TO DO SO. WITH KIND REGARDS I WISH YOU A SAFE RETURN. YOURS TRULY – ROALD AMUNDSEN.'

Letter left by Amunsden in his Polheim tent

'THE POLE. YES, BUT UNDER VERY DIFFERENT CIRCUMSTANCES FROM THOSE EXPECTED... GREAT GOD! THIS IS AN AWFUL PLACE AND TERRIBLE ENOUGH FOR US TO HAVE LABOURED TO IT WITHOUT THE REWARD OF PRIORITY.'

Scott's diary, 17 January 1912

Amundsen and his men *proudly view the Norwegian flag at the South Pole before departure. One month later (from left, standing) Oates, Scott and Evans, with (sitting) Bowers and Wilson, display the British flag there. About 10 photographs were organized by Bowers. The film was found at the Last Camp and developed later.*

Homeward Bound

☞ **AFTER ONE DAY'S STAY, SCOTT AND HIS TEAM** turned their backs on the South Pole and began the enormous return trek. Dispirited and drained, they knew that their health had been deteriorating for weeks. Today we know that their rations were too low in terms of energy for strenuous man-hauling hour after hour by at least 4,180 kilojoules (1,000 calories) per day. Their refined food, with little fibre or roughage, played havoc with their digestion. They would have suffered several vitamin deficiencies, including lack of vitamin A possibly leading to skin problems, and would have been in danger from vitamin C deficiency though there is no mention of anyone suffering from scurvy. Since the Polar Plateau is far above sea level, with the South Pole itself at an altitude of more than 2,830 metres, they would also have been affected by the altitude, making them feel breathless, dizzy and light-headed.

Taking five men instead of four meant reorganizing food rations and fuel use, and cooking times increased. The leather washers on the paraffin can stoppers cracked in the cold and leaked, and some cans lost almost half their contents. Scott had never really allowed much safety margin. The problems were mounting.

Some time before, Petty Officer Edgar Evans had suffered a cut thumb that did not heal. With all the other health problems, his condition worsened and he was no longer able to haul a sledge. On 17 February, between Mid and Lower Depots on Beardmore Glacier, he collapsed. The men loaded him onto the sledge and pulled him back to the tent where he died overnight. Next morning the remaining four left the Beardmore Glacier and headed out onto the Ross Ice Shelf – the Great Ice Barrier.

Edgar Evans, shown here in *full trekking kit at Cape Evans, was the biggest and strongest of the five men in the final Polar Party. So, in effect, he starved faster than the others throughout the trek. The search party never found his body.*

Last Camp

☞ **AS SCOTT, WILSON, BOWERS AND OATES** struggled to cross the Ross Ice Shelf, they recorded some of the worst conditions of their entire South Pole journey. Much later, analysis of various meteorological records from the time showed that the weather was indeed exceptionally adverse with such conditions occurring only infrequently. By now Oates was suffering from horrendous frostbite, especially to his feet, and he had aggravated a leg wound he had received in 1901 during the Boer War. He could hardly walk, and he knew he was holding up the others. Finally he sacrificed himself by leaving the tent during a blizzard, either on or on the eve of his 32nd birthday, never to return.

From 21 March Scott, Wilson and Bowers did not leave their tent because of a blizzard that lasted for days. Scott knew they were just 20 kilometres from One Ton Depot, and 240 kilometres from the base at Cape Evans. Had the depot been in its original position, at 80°S, they probably would have already reached it. But they were now well past any hope of travel. The men wrote their last letters, diary entries and journal notes. Scott recorded: 'Every day we have been ready to start for our depot 11 miles away, but outside the door of the tent it remains a scene of whirling drift... We shall stick it out to the end, but we are getting weaker, of course, and the end cannot be far. It seems a pity, but I do not think I can write more. R. Scott. ... For God's sake look after our people.'

> ❛ "I AM JUST GOING OUTSIDE AND MAY BE SOME TIME." HE WENT OUT INTO THE BLIZZARD AND WE HAVE NOT SEEN HIM SINCE.❜
>
> **Scott's diary, 16 or 17 March 1912**

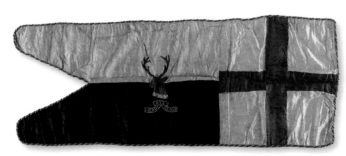

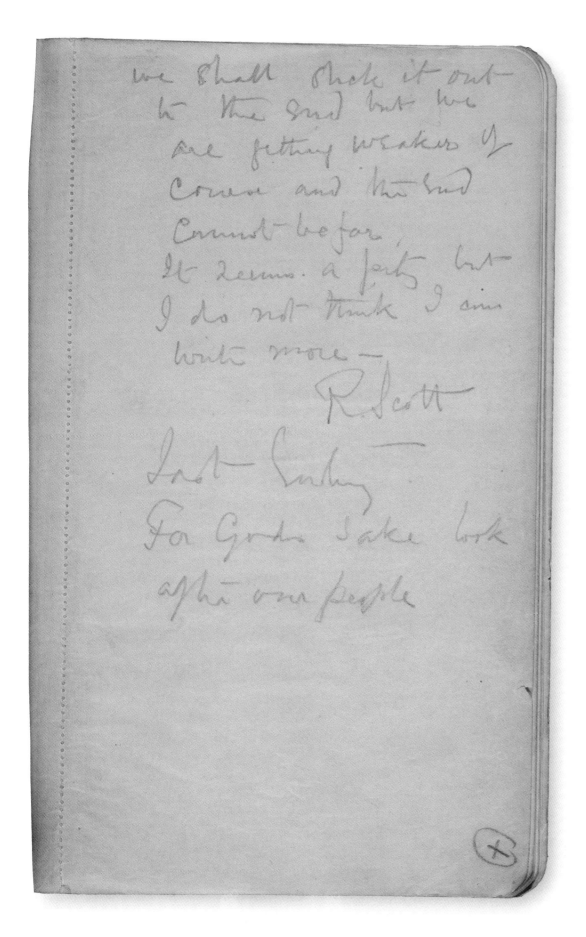

we shall stick it out
to the end but we
are getting weaker of
course and the end
cannot be far.

It seems a pity but
I do not think I can
write more —

R Scott

Last entry.
For Gods sake look
after our people

Sledging flags celebrated
the owner's nationality and were personalized with small embroidered or embossed words and pictures. Scott's silk flag, taken to the South Pole and back, has 'Ready, Aye, Ready'.

Scott's sledging diaries
contain most of the information we know today about the South Pole march and the return journey. Of all the Polar Party, he recorded the most copious notes and kept writing to the very end. Here is his last entry from 29 March 1912.

'It is the Tent.'

☞ **OVER THE PREVIOUS MONTHS,** Scott had given detailed instructions about who should be in command, the resupply of depots with food and fuel and equipment, how and when relief groups should be sent out to meet the Polar Party on their return, and what to do if they did not materialize. On 4 March Cherry-Garrard and Gerof arrived at One Ton Depot and waited for a week, hoping to welcome and aid the party. Running low on supplies, on 10 March they left. It was one week before Oates died, and Scott with his three companions were in a tent just 80 kilometres away.

On 26 March 1912, as winter arrived, Atkinson and Keohane trekked south to search for the missing men, but the weather was too severe. On 30 March they turned back, 160 kilometres from the Last Camp, knowing that the Polar Party had probably now all perished. This was quite possibly the same day that they died.

THE INNER TENT IN WHICH CAPTAIN SCOTT AND HIS TWO COMPANIONS WERE DISCOVERED

This illustration is from a direct photograph taken by a member of the relief party which found Captain Scott's tent on November 12, 1912. The view shows the inner lining of the tent supported on its poles. Commander Evans in his despatch from Christchurch, New Zealand, on February 13 last, said that "the search party found the tent half covered with snow. The sledge with the gear was completely covered, the tent was well spread, and the inner tent was in place on the poles. The bodies were identified, the inner tent was placed over them, and a large cairn of snow was erected"

On 30 October 1912 winter had receded sufficiently for another search party. Just past One Ton Depot, on 12 November, they found the Last Camp. The searchers were devastated to find the bodies of their friends and colleagues. Atkinson examined the three. Scott was in the middle, his arm over Wilson, suggesting Scott died last. The searchers gathered up the records, personal effects, scientific instruments and samples, wrapped the bodies in their outer tent, and erected a snow cairn on top. Then they trekked, deep in mourning, back to base. Atkinson wrote in his official report: '... Alone in their greatness they will lie without change or bodily decay, with the most fitting tomb in the world above them.'

The inner tent of the Last
Camp is pictured after the outer layer had been removed as a burial shroud. Below is the cairn. The cigar box was taken to the South Pole by Scott but never opened.

Among the 16 kilograms
of rock specimens at the Last Camp were (from top) pegmatite, oolitic limestone and coal, indicating a once warm and lush Antarctica.

Legacies

☞ **SCOTT'S SKIS MADE THE ROUND TRIP TO THE POLE** and back –
Gran wore them on their return to Cape Evans, having left his own at
the Last Camp as a memorial cross. As *Terra Nova* left in late January
1913, a three-metre-tall jarrah-wood cross was erected on Observation
Hill, overlooking McMurdo Sound. It commemorates the deaths of
the Polar Party members with an inscription from Tennyson's *Ulysses*:
'To strive, to seek, to find, and not to yield.'

The scientific legacies of the *Terra Nova* expedition are still evident a
century later. The science of glaciology was in its infancy, and the *Terra
Nova* studies expanded its scope by recording how ice slid on land as
glaciers, then floated on the sea as an ice shelf, and cracked off in sections
as icebergs. Because the expedition stayed for so long, over two years, they
were able to track some ice movements for all of that time and obtain longer-
term information than on previous expeditions. It produced the longest
unbroken record of meteorological data taken in Antarctica and Simpson,
the meteorologist, developed several significant theories about Antarctic
weather patterns including ideas to explain why the Antarctic summer
is so much colder than the Arctic's.

Thousands of specimens of animals, plants, rocks and fossils
were collected and are now housed in institutions such as the
Natural History Museum, London, and Canterbury Museum, New
Zealand. New species were discovered and some named after
expedition members. They also found certain fossils known to
be characteristic of southern hemisphere continents, such as
the plant *Glossopteris indica*, which lent support to the
concept of Gondwana. Discoveries like this were
key to the development of ideas about continental
drift, now part of the theory of plate tectonics.

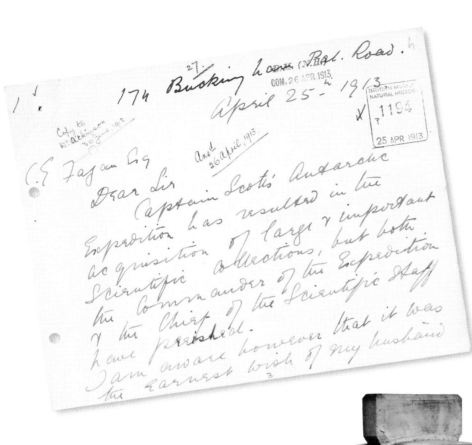

New species of shellfish *discovered by the* Terra Nova *team included this ark shell* Arca novae-zealandiae, *a type of cold-water clam.*

This rock (opposite *middle) contains a fossil of* Glossopteris, *a type of extinct tree-fern. The rocks that Scott and his Polar Party hauled back included fossils of Glossopteris.*

Specimens of the lichen Buellia frigida *preserved in rock. Lichens are among the commonest organisms on cold Antarctic rocks. They are combinations of fungi (moulds) with either algae (simple plants) or cyanobacteria (blue-green algae).*

Kathleen Scott's letter to *the Natural History Museum advises that '…it was the earnest wish of my husband that some similar arrangement be made…as led to such excellent results regarding the geological and biological results from Captain Scott's former* [Discovery] *expedition.'*

This jar (far left) contains a *feather-star* Promachocrinus kerguelensis, *a relative of starfishes. Previously thought to be rare,* the Terra Nova expedition *showed it was numerous and widespread.*

The *Terra Nova* specimen *of deepwater fish from which the new species* Pogonophryne scotti *was described. Its specific name* scotti *commemorates the expedition's leader.*

Afterlives

☞ **AFTER HIS TRIUMPH AT THE SOUTH POLE,** Roald Amundsen continued exploring. He attempted the Northeast Passage along northern Asia, then crossed the North Pole in the airship *Norge*. In 1928 whilst in a search party looking for another airship, his aircraft was lost in the Barents Sea.

Most notable among personal post-*Terra Nova* accounts was Cherry-Garrard's *Worst Journey in the World*, 1922. This described not just his 'Winter Journey' to obtain emperor penguin eggs but many other aspects of the expedition. Cherry-Garrard suffered mental health problems later in life and was haunted by the memory that while he was waiting at One Ton Depot, Scott with his companions were in their tent perhaps only three days' journey away.

'I LEAVE CAPE EVANS WITH NO REGRET. I NEVER WANT TO SEE THE PLACE AGAIN. THE PLEASANT MEMORIES ARE ALL SWALLOWED UP IN THE BAD ONES.'

Apsley Cherry-Garrard

Edward Evans, second-in-command of *Terra Nova*, had almost died on his return with the South Pole support party. In July 1913 Lashly and Crean each received the Albert Medal for saving him. Evans went on to have an illustrious naval career and rose to become an admiral.

Several *Terra Nova* scientists achieved great distinction. George Simpson became the longest-serving Director of the Meteorological Office, serving from 1920 to 1938. Geologist Frank Debenham was instrumental in founding the Scott Polar Research Institute and served as director until 1946. Another of the Institute's founders was Raymond Priestley, who held varied high-ranking academic posts in Britain and Australia. T. Griffith Taylor also rose to senior positions, including first President of the Institute of Australian Geographers in 1959.

Gran, Thomas Williamson,
Edward Nelson and Crean, part of the 1912 Southern Party under the overall command of Atkinson, who went to look for, and found, Scott and his companions.

Ponting took many intimate *portraits of the men, here highlighting Cherry-Garrard's youthful innocence. Cherry-Garrard lived to know that, sadly, his 'Worst Journey' for penguin eggs produced no major scientific advance. Even as the eggs were gathered, the penguin theory of bird evolution was gradually being discounted.*

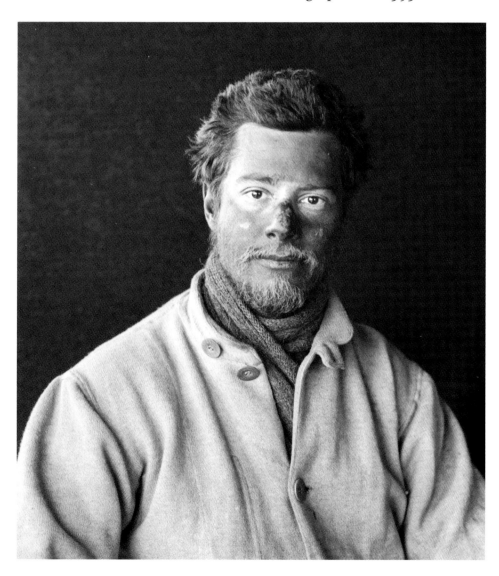

Perspectives

☞ **NEWS OF THE SOUTH POLE CONQUEST** and Scott's fate broke on 10 February 1913 when *Terra Nova* reached New Zealand. Kathleen Scott heard as she herself was travelling there. Had her husband survived, he would doubtless have received a knighthood. Kathleen was awarded the rank of a widow of a Knight Commander of the Order of the Bath. She became a successful sculptor and remarried in 1922. Scott's son Peter rose to fame as a naturalist, conservationist, bird expert and artist.

Until the 1960s the epic reputation of 'Scott of the Antarctic' held firm. Then commentators began to delve behind the established myths. Criticisms surfaced about Scott as a man, officer and leader, based partly on accounts of *Terra Nova* expedition members. Compared to Amundsen's thorough planning and preparations, Scott was accused of sailing close to the wind, leaving little safety margin for problems, taking some decisions on the spur of the moment and not always consulting his colleagues. For example, why did he decide to take five men to the South Pole, rather than the orginally planned four? He was also criticized for not revealing his ideas until the last moment, so his men were in the dark and could not prepare mentally and physically for what was demanded of them.

However the past few decades have seen spirited defences of Scott the man which, while acknowledging some personal failings, have restored his reputation as one of the giants of exploration. Scott's skills as a writer, chronicler and documenter have never been questioned, though he often wrote with posterity in mind.

'FOR MY OWN SAKE I DO NOT REGRET THIS JOURNEY, WHICH HAS SHOWN THAT ENGLISHMEN CAN ENDURE HARDSHIPS, HELP ONE ANOTHER, AND MEET DEATH WITH AS GREAT A FORTITUDE AS EVER IN THE PAST.'

Scott's Message to the Public

The Polar Medal was *instituted by Edward VII for outstanding service in the Arctic and Antarctic. This replaced the earlier Arctic Medal. The first Polar Medal was to Scott as leader of the* Discovery *expedition, 1901–04. Scott posthumously received a second bar for the* Terra Nova *expedition.*

Scott's bicorne hat, part *of his official Royal Navy Commander uniform, was one of many items he left at home, which have since become treasured memorials to his achievements.*

The Scott Memorial in *Christchurch, New Zealand, shows him fully rigged and resolute against Antarctic rigours. It was sculpted by his wife Kathleen and erected in 1917. Christchurch today is 'Gateway to the Antarctic' and main base for more than 100 flights each year to McMurdo Sound. The memorial was damaged in the Christchurch earthquake of 22 February 2011.*

21st Century

☛ **ANTARCTICA IS STILL THE COLDEST, WINDIEST, MOST REMOTE**, most challenging, least visited place on Earth. If Scott could return today, he might well be surprised by the Amundsen–Scott South Pole Station, established in 1956. Its inhabitants number from 50 through winter to 200-plus in summer and study a vast array of scientific topics. Scott might then return to Cape Evans and visit McMurdo Station, the largest

Antarctic base with three airstrips, 100 buildings and facilities for 1,300 people. His old *Terra Nova* hut, as well as Shackleton's *Nimrod* hut, are places of pilgrimage and immense historical significance. Until recently at risk of loss, both are part of the New Zealand Antarctic Heritage Trust's Ross Sea Heritage Restoration Project, a world-leading, international polar conservation project to save both the sites and their extensive artefact collections for the benefit of the international community.

What might also amaze Scott is how the data collected by the *Terra Nova* expedition are critical to current researches such as global warming and atmospheric pollution. Not only have Scott and *Terra Nova* earned an esteemed place in world history and the annals of adventure, they also left a considerable scientific legacy.

Cold, dry conditions have *kept the Cape Evans hut in an astonishing condition of preservation. This modern photograph shows the wardroom table, harnesses and provisions piled high – a century after the hut bustled with laughter, tears, high hopes, and finally dashed dreams.*

Key Events

1909
Scott sets about raising funds for a new expedition to the South Pole

15 JUNE 1910
Terra Nova sets sail from Cardiff

29 NOVEMBER 1910
Terra Nova leaves Port Chalmers, New Zealand for Antarctica

EARLY JANUARY 1911
Terra Nova arrives in the McMurdo Sound

17 JANUARY 1911
Cape Evans hut ready for occupation

JANUARY 1911
Depot laying for South Pole trek begins

27 JANUARY 1911
First Western Geological Party (Taylor, Debenham, Wright and Edgar Evans) dropped at Butter Point by *Terra Nova*. Then *Terra Nova* heads with the Eastern Party eastwards

3 FEBRUARY 1911
Meeting of the *Terra Nova* and *Fram* in the Bay of Whales

9 FEBRUARY 1911
Terra Nova leaves Cape Evans for New Zealand to avoid being frozen in

20 FEBRUARY 1911
Terra Nova drops what was the Eastern Party and is now the Northern Party (Campbell, Dickason, Priestley, Levick, Browning and Abbott) at Cape Adare

13 APRIL 1911
First Western Geological Party arrive back at Cape Evans

27 JUNE 1911
Wilson, Bowers and Cherry-Garrard set off on the 'Worst Journey in the World' to Cape Crozier in search of emperor penguin eggs

1 AUGUST 1911
Wilson, Bowers and Cherry-Garrard arrive back at Cape Evans

LATE OCTOBER – EARLY NOVEMBER 1911
Scott's contingent of 16 men sets off on South Pole trek

17 NOVEMBER 1911
Second Western Geological Party (Taylor, Debenham, Gran and Forde) reach Butter Point and walk on to Granite Harbour

14 DECEMBER 1911
Amundsen reaches South Pole

21 DECEMBER 1911
Support party (Cherry-Garrard, Atkinson, Wright and Keohane) set off back to Cape Evans

4 JANUARY 1912
Support party (Edward Evans, Crean and Lashly) set off back to Cape Evans

EARLY JANUARY 1912
Terra Nova picks up Northern Party and takes them to Evans Coves, 320 kilometres from Cape Evans

17 JANUARY 1912
Polar Party (Scott, Oates, Edgar Evans, Bowers and Wilson) reach the South Pole

18 FEBRUARY 1912
Edgar Evans dies en route back to Cape Evans

4 MARCH 1912
Cherry-Garrard and Gerof arrive at One Ton Depot hoping to help the Polar Party and leave on 10 March as supplies are running low

7 MARCH 1912
Amundsen announces reaching South Pole on arrival in Hobart, Australia

16–17 MARCH 1912
Oates steps out of the tent in a blizzard and is never seen again

26 MARCH 1912
Atkinson and Keohane trek south to find the Polar Party but turn back on 30 March as the weather is too severe

30 MARCH 1912
Possibly the day that the surviving Polar Party die

30 OCTOBER 1912
A search party goes out to look for the Polar Party

7 NOVEMBER 1912
The Northern Party arrive back at Cape Evans after surviving a second Antarctic winter and a six-week trek

12 NOVEMBER 1912
Search party under Atkinson finds the Last Camp and Scott, Bowers and Wilson

10 FEBRUARY 1913
News announced that Scott's Polar Party reached the South Pole but died on the return

14 FEBRUARY 1913
Service to commemorate Polar Party at St Paul's Cathedral, London

Index

Picture Credits

© New Zealand Antarctic Heritage Trust
p.3 left; p.13 top left & right; p.18; p.24 top; p.25 top; p.26 bottom right; p.33 top; p.34 top; p.59 bottom; p.60; p.63 top left; pp.68-69 bottom; p.70 top; p.71 top.

© Canterbury Museum, New Zealand
p.3 middle 19XX.4.472; p.3 right 2010.10.2; p.4 Maull & Fox photogravure, 19XX.2.5103; p.13 bottom, MS127; p.15 bottom G Hillsdon photograph, Kinsey collection, 1940.193.204; p.16 H Ponting photograph, 19XX.2.5088; p.21 H Ponting photograph, Pennell collection, 1975.289.9; p.22 H Ponting photograph, Pennell collection, 1975.289.16; p.23 H Ponting photograph, 19XX.2.5076; p.24 top, 19XX.4.464, bottom, 1970.67.1; p.25 bottom right, 1999.79.1, bottom left, A179.29; p.26 top, LTR, 1977.148.1, 1976.476.1, 2010.40.4, 2010.40.1, bottom left, Welsh Tin Plate and Metal Stamping Co, 1983.180.2; p.27 top left, Walker & Hall Ltd, 2010.105.1, top right, Walker & Hall Ltd, 2010.105.3, bottom, H Ponting photograph, 19XX.2.5073; p.28 19XX.4.472; p.29 H Ponting photograph, Pennell collection, 1975.289.68; pp.30–31 top, Messrs. Mendleberg, 19XX.4.457; p.30 right, The Wolsey, 19XX.4.66, bottom, 1980.219.1; p.31 top, 1968.57.11, bottom, Pophams, 19XX.4.458; p.32 H Ponting photograph, 19XX.2.5077; p.33 left, 1975.293.24, right, Wallace Triangle, 1975.233.5, bottom, 1983.180.10; p.35 top, S Paton letter, 2004.77.1, middle, De Larue & Co Ltd playing cards, Whitford collection, 2008.36.12,

bottom, 19XX.2.5089; p.36 top, Smith, Elder & Co London, Skellerup collection, LIBA193, bottom, H Ponting photograph, Pennell collection, 1975.289.107; p.37 left, E Nelson menu, 2008.70.1, middle, 1967.113.5, right, 1975.284.52; p.39 right, 1977.105.1; p.40 Spencer Buffalo, 1988.40.1; p.44 19XX.2.5079; p.45 left, 2009.27.2, right, Herbert G Ponting, 2009.27.1; p.46 Ackerman & Co, 2010.110.1; p.48 top, A182.20, middle, A182.19, bottom, George de Lacy & Son, A182.21; p.49 top, E Evans letter, Morris collection, MS178, bottom, H Ponting photograph, Pennell collection, 1975.289.35; p.55 top left, 19XX.4.462; p.57 H Ponting photograph, 19XX.2.5094; p.58 bottom, A176.50; p.61 bottom, H Ponting photograph, Pennell collection, 1975.289.48; p.62 left, H Ponting photograph, Pennell collection, 1975.289.108; p.63 right, 19XX.4.3470, bottom left, LTR, 1968.59.139, 1968.59.40, 1968.57.13; p.64 Kinsey collection, 1924.82.1; p.68 top, The Wolsey, 2006.9.1; p.69 top, 2010.10.2, middle, 1969.297.1, bottom, 1977.345.3; p.73 top, 1977.71.3; p.74 top, 19XX.4.131; p.75 top, Messrs Burroughs & Wellcome, 19XX.4.135; pp.76–77 bottom, 2005.184.1; p.76 top, 19XX.4.431; p.77 top left, W D and H O Wills, 1968.57.29, middle, 1967.113.4, right, New Zealand Alpine Club Inc collection, 1955.91.3; p.80 H Ponting photograph, Pennell collection, 1975.289.114; p.84 top, 1967.128.22; p.85 19XX.2.5093; p.89 H Ponting photograph, 19XX.2.5092; p.90 top, The Royal Mint, 1948.85.3, bottom, 1948.85.1.

© Illustrated London News Ltd/Mary Evans
p.5, p.7, p.65, p.84 bottom
© Mary Evans / Grenville Collins Postcard Collection p.12 top
© Mary Evans Picture Library p.12 bottom, p.78,

Licensed with permission of the Scott Polar Research Institute, University of Cambridge
p.19, p.51 top, bottom, p.54, p.56, p.61 top, pp.70-71 bottom, p.72, pp.72-73 bottom; pp.74-75 bottom, p.79, p.88

pp.8-9 Photo: Nick Powell (National Science Foundation); p.11 top left and right public domain (from the collection of the National Maritime Museum, London); p.11 bottom public domain; p.15 top public domain; p19 bottom right Land Design Studio; p.21 top Land Design Studio after plan provided by New Zealand Antarctic Heritage Trust; p.34 bottom courtesy EMI Group Archive Trust, photo: Hannah Hempstead; p.53 © The Art Archive/Culver Pictures; p.62 right excerpt from *The Worst Journey in the World* by Apsley Cherry-Garrard by permission of the Scott Polar Research Institute, University of Cambridge; p.82 © National Maritime Museum, Greenwich, London. Acquired with assistance from the Heritage Lottery Fund; p.83 Photo © The British Library Board. By permission of the estate of R F Scott; p.91 © Claver Carroll/Photolibrary; pp.92-93 © Jane Ussher.

All other images © NHMPL, The Natural History Museum Picture Library